A Library Worker's Guide to Saying No to White Supremacy Work Culture

A Library Worker's Guide to Saying No to White Supremacy Work Culture

Christina Fuller-Gregory

BLOOMSBURY ACADEMIC
NEW YORK • LONDON • OXFORD • NEW DELHI • SYDNEY

BLOOMSBURY ACADEMIC

Bloomsbury Publishing Inc, 1359 Broadway, New York, NY 10018, USA
Bloomsbury Publishing Plc, 50 Bedford Square, London, WC1B 3DP, UK
Bloomsbury Publishing Ireland, 29 Earlsfort Terrace, Dublin 2, D02 AY28, Ireland

BLOOMSBURY, BLOOMSBURY ACADEMIC and the Diana logo are trademarks of
Bloomsbury Publishing Plc

First published in the United States of America 2025

Copyright © Bloomsbury Publishing, Inc., 2025

Cover Design by Diana Nuhn
Cover images:
© istock.com / Olena Zagoruyko

All rights reserved. No part of this publication may be: i) reproduced or transmitted in any form, electronic or mechanical, including photocopying, recording or by means of any information storage or retrieval system without prior permission in writing from the publishers; or ii) used or reproduced in any way for the training, development or operation of artificial intelligence (AI) technologies, including generative AI technologies. The rights holders expressly reserve this publication from the text and data mining exception as per Article 4(3) of the Digital Single Market Directive (EU) 2019/790.

Bloomsbury Publishing Inc does not have any control over, or responsibility for, any third-party websites referred to or in this book. All internet addresses given in this book were correct at the time of going to press. The author and publisher regret any inconvenience caused if addresses have changed or sites have ceased to exist, but can accept no responsibility for any such changes.

Library of Congress Cataloging-in-Publication Data Available

ISBN: HB: 978-1-5381-9312-9
PB: 978-1-5381-9313-6
ePDF: 979-8-7651-5411-3
eBook: 978-1-5381-9314-3

Typeset by Deanta Global Publishing Services, Chennai, India
Printed and bound in the United States of America

For product safety related questions contact productsafety@bloomsbury.com.

To find out more about our authors and books visit www.bloomsbury.com and sign up for our newsletters.

Contents

Acknowledgments vi

Part 1 Introducing White Supremacy Work Culture 1

1. Introducing White Supremacy Work Culture 3
2. An Organizational Culture of Perfectionism 13
3. All the Write Words 21
4. No Time to Spare 29
5. The Way It's Always Been Done 39

Part 2 A Practice in Reflection 47

6. The Myth of Professionalism 51
7. No Conflict Please 55
8. Defensive Maneuvers 63
9. Stretched and Stressed 71

Part 3 Shifting Our Views of Professionalism 79

10. Showing Up Authentically 83
11. No "I" in Team 87
12. Honoring Complexity 93
13. The Comfort of Privilege 99
14. Our Path Forward 107

Appendix 113
Index 118
About the Author 121

Acknowledgments

In memory of Valerie Rowe-Jackson: your leadership inspired me, your mentorship empowered me, and your kindness saved me.

PART 1

Introducing White Supremacy Work Culture

1 Introducing White Supremacy Work Culture

I've always enjoyed reading books that start with "if you're reading this book." What always follows are the multitude of reasons that reading the book will change your life or way of thinking for the better. It is with a similar hope that I write this book. If you are reading *A Library Worker's Guide to Saying No to White Supremacy Work Culture*, then you're:

☐ Ready to acknowledge, address, and redress the ways in which white supremacy culture exists in your library.

☐ Prepared to challenge the professional behaviors that we've long held as the standards of excellence.

☐ Excited to create a more inclusive and culturally proficient working environment, believing that libraries are dynamic institutions that can (and should) exist beyond the historical and foundational.

Did you check all of the boxes above? What about just one? Even if you aren't yet able to check a box above, the fact that you've started reading is a tremendous step forward on your journey toward saying no to white supremacy work culture. And, before we begin, I want to be clear that this book is not about shaming or blaming. The purpose of this book is rooted in what I call the three A's: **awareness**, **accountability**, and **action**.

Throughout the book, I will ask you to practice **awareness** by thinking deeply about those aspects of white supremacy work culture that you recognize. Recognition of a thing is equally important to addressing that thing. It will be important to note those moments in which you see yourself or your organization reflected in a described example or behavior. You may also want to develop awareness around those examples that may feel foreign to you, because learning about how the aspects of white supremacy work culture present will help you to better understand how they manifest. Another key component of engaging in this process is cultivating an **accountability** practice. When describing what happens when we build awareness, I mentioned the importance of seeing how our individual or organizational behaviors have been informed by white supremacy work culture. Accountability allows us to level up from recognition to responsibility. You may start by considering those systemic behaviors that have long been excused as unique to our organization, thinking about not only what they are, but how you address them.

Accountability often requires us to "tell on ourselves," acting as truth tellers in service of explicitly calling forth those instances of white supremacy work culture that you've participated in or silently approved. I'll ask that you approach accountability in two ways: (1) individual accountability, those ideas that you have the power to actualize or control, and (2) organizational accountability, those ideas that must be owned, led, introduced, and supported on an organizational level.

And finally, **action**. Action is one of my favorite steps because it allows us to use the information gathered from building capacity in both awareness and accountability to fully realize our efforts and inform tangible change.

In writing circles, there are three parts of a book that are critical to drawing in the reader; they are called "the first slap, the second slap, and the climax." As we consider and compare the significance of the three A's to the most vital pieces of a book, think of awareness as the first slap or the first pivotal point in your journey. **What is your organizational story? What might you learn from it?** Accountability is the second slap. The second slap generally requires a turning point or deeper examination of a situation; the same can be said as you engage in the accountability phase. **What is your accountability turning point? In what ways will it inform deeper examination, consideration, or care?** The reason, however, that we continue reading any good book is the climax, where the character unflinchingly faces their most important challenge. While you're not a "character" you are an invested participant, and your fearlessness in approaching any "challenges" presented by this content will inform your **actions** going forward. It is the point at which you're able to take the vital information you learn about yourself and your organization, use it to inform a deeper examination of what could be, and finally take the steps needed to face the often uncomfortable act of instituting change.

Step 1: Awareness

Recognizing how what we know about ourselves and our organizations informs our behaviors.

To prepare for the work ahead, let's start with a bit of awareness around how white supremacy culture came to exist in our libraries. **Ready for a little history lesson?**

It was not without a hard-fought effort that libraries as we know them today became a reality. In 1896, the Supreme Court handed down a landmark ruling called Plessy vs. Ferguson. Before there was Rosa Parks who refused to give up her seat, there was Homer Plessy, an activist and man of color in Louisiana, who alongside other community activists of color called the Committee of Citizens, decided to peacefully protest the Separate Car Act of 1892. What Plessy and the Committee of Citizens believed to be a rightful and just protest against an act that would require people of color to sit in different trains would be the foundation for a landmark decision by the Supreme Court that "racial segregation laws did not violate the US Constitution as long as the facilities for each race were equal in quality."[1] This decision became what we now know today as "separate but equal." The agonizing contradiction of this decision was that while things remained "separate," the infrastructure provided to people of color was decidedly not equal. If anything, it was separate and inferior. What this meant for public spaces, including libraries, was that there was now a recognized and codified law in place that could be used to wholesale justify exclusionary practices. And this was just the beginning.

Even as libraries became more widespread in the early twentieth century through the auspices of businessman and philanthropist Andrew Carnegie, the reality of library services to populations of color, particularly African-Americans, still remained relatively non-existent. This lack of existence did not go unnoticed by African-American educator and scholar W. E. B. Du Bois, who railed against the construction of Carnegie's 1902 public library in Atlanta, Georgia, highlighting that the opening of a segregated library failed to take into consideration the fact that African-Americans comprised "one-third" of the population of the growing, urban city.[2] Dubois' words would go unheeded until some nineteen years later, when Atlanta's first public library serving African Americans would be opened. And while there were outliers, like the

Louisville Western Branch Library, which opened in 1905, the desegregation of libraries would not come for many more years. But, it's important to note that the learning vacuum created in communities through the lack of public library access was often filled through churches, school libraries, and even segregated reading rooms that existed within whites-only libraries.

For libraries, the slow shift toward integration wouldn't become a consideration until Brown v. Board of Education, the Supreme Court case that "established the precedent that 'separate-but-equal' education and other services were not, in fact, equal at all." And even following a Supreme Court ruling mandating that racial segregation end, many public-serving entities, including libraries, outright refused to recognize the decision or moved languidly toward integration. And for the many African-Americans who looked forward to the promise and possibility of a future where we were all created equal, this slow-moving approach to change wrought painful and life-changing consequences.

One such example of this is US representative John Lewis, who in 2017 reflected upon a deeply painful experience in which he and his family attempted to register for library cards in his home state of Alabama. Upon arrival, he was met by a librarian who told them that the library was for "white's only, not coloreds."[3] Imagine the impact of having a world of books within reach, only to be told that the color of his skin was the singular barrier that prevented access. By his own admission, this experience in 1956 so deeply impacted him that he didn't return to a library until 1998.

One of the most catalyzing moments for library integration came through the efforts of the Tougaloo Nine, a group of African-American college students at Tougaloo College[4] who were also members of the Jackson Youth Council of the National Association for the Advancement of Colored People (NAACP). In 1961, they organized and staged a peaceful read-in protest at the Main Library in Jackson, Mississippi. Although the protest ended with the Tougaloo Nine being arrested, charged, and sentenced to thirty days in jail and fined $100 (the jail sentence was stayed on the condition that the students participate in no further protests), their efforts provided the NAACP with the grounds they needed to file a class-action lawsuit against Jackson Public Library. And while the Tougaloo Nine received outsized punishment for their efforts, Jackson Public Library was ordered to desegregate less than a year later, in 1962.

While this isn't an exhaustive timeline of the many events that shaped the story of our libraries, these moments in history provide a touchpoint into the complicated past that libraries have with colonialism, racism, and segregation. Early twentieth-century libraries played just as critical a role in the implementation of separate but equal as other public-serving entities, a challenging realization to understand and unpack. It almost feels uncomfortable to imagine our role in operationalizing and supporting an ideal that ensured access would most certainly be inequitable. But sitting with and in the discomfort of this realization will act as a powerful tool that you, as library workers, must use to develop a sense of awareness around the libraries roles in creating environments that were counter to the narrative of welcome. With this awareness comes insights into the systems, policies, and people who have created the underpinnings of the library as we know it to be.

> **Conversational Prompt: Challenge Your Awareness**
>
> 1. If asked, what could you tell someone about the history of your library?
> 2. As an organization, how often do you discuss your history?
> 3. Are there long-standing practices, rooted in your library's history, that still exist in your organization? What are they?

Step 2: Accountability

Owning the ways in which the behaviors we exhibit, witness, or silently condone are ancillary contributors to a systemic problem.

What John Lewis experienced in that library in 1956 is what we know today as white supremacy culture. White supremacy culture centers the idea that while,

> Culture reflects the beliefs, values, norms, and standards of a group, a community, a town, a state, a nation. White supremacy culture is the widespread ideology baked into the beliefs, values, norms, and standards of our groups (many if not most of them), our communities, our towns, our states, our nation, teaching us both overtly and covertly that whiteness holds value, whiteness is value.[5]

Within the framework of the construct of white supremacy we see "respected" standards related to professionalism, success, hiring and retention, socialization, and communication style determined and enforced through a lens that was designed by and for white people. What we lose in the practice of this ideology are the diverse, authentic, or unique perspectives of those individuals who have been taught that their value isn't necessarily the "desired" value that those who hold positions of power are looking for.

The idea of white supremacy culture was first introduced in 1999 by Dr. Tema Okun. Okun's seminal paper "White Supremacy Culture" discussed fifteen characteristics that may be introduced by individuals or organizations through behaviors. Using Okun's work as inspiration, this book will examine white supremacy culture in the working environment, specifically in libraries. Each of the following chapters is dedicated to taking an unfiltered look at the fifteen aspects of what we will reference going forward as white supremacy *work* culture. As you are introduced to characteristics, behaviors, and ideas that are unique to each of the aspects, I invite you to consider how your own professional origin story has been informed or shaped by white supremacy work culture.

Believe it or not, remnants of a past that attributed professional value to a set of clearly defined practices still exist. Failing to acknowledge the existence of these practices, attempting to maintain them as ever-present parts of our library narrative, or denying the existence of the echoes of white supremacy work culture that are still very much present in many of our organizations is counterintuitive, distracting us from what our libraries could be. If we want to create an internal culture rooted in authentic change, it's time to begin by examining our fixed mindsets[6] and those things that we've been told are "precious" to our organization. Let's start by thinking about how our individual and collective behaviors inform our internal practices.

> **Conversational Prompt: Owning Our Behaviors**
> 1. What organizational values (overt or covert) may be teaching that whiteness holds value, whiteness is value?
> 2. In what ways have you exhibited, witnessed, or silently contributed to white supremacy work culture?
> 3. What policies, procedures, or services are considered "precious" in your organization?

Step 3: Action: Awareness + Accountability = Change

There is an order to the process of engaging the three A's. While I'd love to say that action alone could help you to begin the work of addressing white supremacy work culture, that wouldn't be true. And much of the work of becoming an individual or organization that understands the need for these efforts involves an ability to speak truth to power. The fact is that action without the information and resources provided by building awareness and cultivating accountability is tantamount to performative activism. It is, in effect, walking around your library with a megaphone shouting "we need change now." without doing any of the work needed to create substantive change.

In reading this book, you'll find that each step is reliant upon the other, an interconnectedness created to ensure that you're individually and collectively able to create a well-thought-out work plan. As an introduction to the work ahead, you'll find that this chapter includes both conversation prompts and an Action Exercise. The prompts are designed to support you in building your awareness and accountability, and the Action Exercises are designed to reinforce your discoveries.

Are you ready to say no to white supremacy work culture? Let's get to work!

Action Exercise: What's My Organizational History?

Directions: The purpose of this exercise is to create an organizational roadmap of your library's history. Understanding the history of libraries and past segregation, colonization, and so on. To know who you are today requires you to know how you began.

Tip: If working in a group, I encourage you to complete the Action Exercises individually, following up to discuss your findings with the larger group. If reading this book for yourself, use the conversation prompts to inform your personal growth.

1. When were we founded? By whom?

   _____
   _____
   _____

2. What is our organization's desegregation story? Who was instrumental in this effort?

   _____
   _____
   _____

3. When did we begin authentically welcoming BIPOC (Black, Indigenous, and People of Color) into our library? Consider milestones in representation related to hiring/recruitment/advancement, programming efforts, collections, and services.

   _____
   _____
   _____

4. How has the cultural topography of our staff changed over the years?

   _____
   _____
   _____

5. What were the original policies of our organization? How do they track with what we offer as policy today?

   _____
   _____
   _____

Notes

1   Plessy v Ferguson, 1896.
2   Brown v. Board of Education, 1954.
3   John Lewis, "Note to Self," *CBS News*, June 29, 2017, https://www.cbsnews.com/video/note-to-self-congressman-john-lewis/.

4 W. A. Wiegand, "Desegregating Libraries in the American South," *ALA Magazine*, 48, no. 6: (2017, June): 32–37.
5 "White Supremacy Culture." www.whitesupremacyculture.info.
6 C. Dweck, *Mindset* (London: Robinson, an imprint of Constable & Robinson Ltd, 2017).

2 An Organizational Culture of Perfectionism

White Supremacy Work Culture Characteristic: Perfectionism

> **Implications of Perfectionism**
> - An environment that relies upon shame, blame, or fear to inspire effort
> - Regularly acknowledging the efforts and work of those who already hold the most power (whether they did the work or not)
> - Persistently calling out what's wrong but rarely what's right
> - An expected sense of "vocational awe" without recognition of boundaries or staff burnout
> - Mistakes being viewed as wholly negative

When you consider the idea of perfectionism, what comes to mind? Do you immediately think of words such as excellence, flawless, or mistake-free? While these words invoke the desired impact of perfectionism, there are many others that often accompany this practice—words such as inflexibility or anxiety. The language we use around a behavior often helps us to better frame our ideas and actions, so I share the language and wording associated with perfectionism with you early on in this chapter, so that you can begin to think about the dichotomy of the idea of perfectionism and, perhaps, you'll develop your own supporting language to define what happens to (and around) us when we allow our desire to maintain impossibly high standards to take front in center in our libraries.

> What other words or ideas pull forward for you? List them here.

Perfectionism plays a critical role in white supremacy work culture. It informs many of the professional constructs to which we've become accustomed. Perfectionisms' impacts on the working environment run so deeply that language has been developed around it. Sayings like "going the extra mile," "paying your dues," or "burning the midnight oil" have been normalized in our everyday conversations as signals of our learned behaviors around working toward a goal of perfection.

For library workers, an emphasis on doing things just right has inspired a "more is more" library culture in which we feel we are only as successful as our workloads, committee engagements, approaches to collection development, or organizational statistics. The practice of perfection shows up in many different ways. On an individual level, it may emerge as saying "yes" to professional requests, fearful that in saying "no" the door to opportunity will be forever closed. Organizationally, the quest for perfection may lead to a toxic working environment where progress is measured and determined through behaviors that rely upon shaming and blaming staff to inspire effort.

There are also many other indicators of perfectionism that show up in our libraries, having both organizational and individual ramifications. Examples of these include:

- [ ] Not honoring the efforts of all contributors.
- [ ] An expected sense of "vocational awe" without recognition of boundaries or staff burnout.
- [ ] Mistakes being viewed as wholly negative.
- [ ] A feeling amongst staff that they can "never get it right."
- [ ] Language or behaviors frequently center the importance of "fit" as the standard bearer for organizational excellence.

Did you find any of the above examples familiar? Perhaps they are current or past behaviors that you recognize as part of your library culture. I invite you to consider the first chapter, where I shared the three A's of counteracting white supremacy work culture—awareness, accountability, and action. This aforementioned list, while not exhaustive, has been shared with you to heighten your sense of awareness and invite you to consider how the singularity of seeking perfection can often have adverse consequences. While the intent of promoting perfection may be to encourage staff to be their very best, the unintended impact often becomes overworked and undervalued employees, and low morale.

But perhaps the most dangerous effect of promoting perfection in our libraries is conflating perfectionism with sameness. In environments where this occurs, the professional worth of a library worker is often reliant upon their ability to discount aspects of their individual identity in favor of mirroring the behaviors, traditions, ideologies, and perspectives of those colleagues who hold the most power. In library spaces, we see ideals of perfection played out in a variety of ways including similar fashion choices, patterns of speech and language, and most detrimentally, bullying or in-group behaviors—all driven by the desire to promote and protect the image of perfection.

Let's take a moment to challenge our awareness of perfectionism in our organizations.

> **Conversational Prompt (Awareness): Perfectionism and Your Organization**
> 1. Consider the indicators of perfectionism shared above. List the behaviors that resonate with you and why.
> 2. Are these past or current organizational behaviors?
> 3. If past, what was done to address or redress the behaviors?
> 4. If present, where is it showing up? What does acknowledging the behaviors require from administration, managers, or staff?

Alongside traits of colonization, we also find that our inclinations toward perfection are an organic byproduct of our long-standing library commitment to professional standards. The standards by which we provide library services are often informed by a desire for perceived positive perception. In our world, positive perception informs community buy-in, funding, resources, and staffing. As library workers, you recognize that there is tremendous pressure that comes with being everything to everyone.

Our work toward the idea of positive perception leads to markers of perfectionism that include an extreme focus on success or a persistent fear of failure. In our libraries, this pursuit of success may present as requiring library workers to act as a monolith—behaving and presenting as a singular unit, maintaining rigid organizational practices, or actively limiting displays of creativity, experimentation, or difference. Before we can address the impacts of perfectionism in our libraries, we first have to acknowledge how it shows up in our spaces.

What professional standards exist in your organizations that were designed to work in service of perceived positive perception? Are they effective? Or, are they straining an already fatigued workforce? As individuals, we combat perfectionism through our willingness to acknowledge why being perfect is important to us, considering how and why we are reflecting our personal need to be seen as valued contributors on our colleagues or teams. Ask yourself, who or what defined my individual perception of perfectionism? You may be surprised by how these ideas have shaped the ways you work or engage with others. If you're concerned about how your perfectionism practice may be impacting your colleagues or team, asking someone you work closely with and trust to act as an accountability partner is a highly effective way to begin identifying those instances in which you are projecting your own need for perfection.

An organizational approach to addressing perfectionism requires the organization to own the internal culture of winning. Start by having an open and honest conversation with your team about failure and mistakes. Ask participants to share their perspectives on your organizational behaviors around mistakes. Will you find that your colleagues or team believe that mistakes in your organization are viewed singularly as threats to success, rather than opportunities for growth? Deepen the discussion by welcoming ideas for developing, introducing, and implementing professional standards that define and ground your organization.

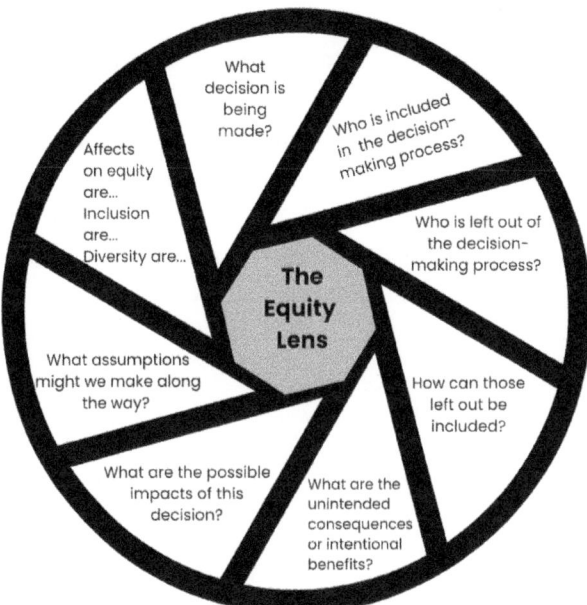

Figure 2.1 *Diagram of the Equity Lens. Source: Christina Fuller-Gregory.*

Professional standards should be developed through an equity lens, with the intention of inviting library workers to contribute to conversations about what thriving, successful, and positively perceived libraries can be. The equity lens diagram, is a dynamic method of applying an evaluative approach to solving issues of equity. Answering the questions introduced through the equity lens individually or collectively will provide you with greater insight into the power structures used to inform the decision-making process. The questions used below are a great place to begin, but you may also develop additional questions that are informed by your knowledge of the current state of your organization's EDI efforts. Within these contexts, there are opportunities to consider ideas or behaviors that challenge or transform the ways that perfectionism is reflected in our professional spaces.

Take a moment to reflect upon your own professional standards and their alignment with perfectionism.

> **Conversational Prompt (Accountability): Perfectionism and Professional Standard**
>
> 1. What are the professional standards of your organization?
> 2. Who in your organization decides what standards of excellence look like?
> 3. Is there a collective and inclusive vision around professional standards? Who is invited to contribute to this conversation?

While perfectionism impacts all library workers, the outcomes of this practice in the working environment have far greater impacts on minoritized, marginalized, or racialized library workers. As with each of the characteristics that we'll discuss throughout the book, the construct of perfectionism, along with the often impossible standards of what is considered perfect, have been determined, constructed, and enforced through systems of white supremacy.

Consider the emotional toll of saying no to an opportunity as one of the few or only members of a marginalized group in your organization. Or the tremendously high expectations that come with being a tokenized member of staff—held to a higher standard or viewed as representative of your entire race. Beyond these examples, they may also experience false narratives around performance or performance reviews that signal that being perfect, or getting as close to it as possible, may be the path toward advancement. Conversely, when unable to demonstrate the behaviors that are organizationally tied to perfection, minoritized, marginalized, or racialized library workers may be subject to the levying of greater consequences. I liken this to an actor who is asked to perform a part without being made aware of their character's backstory. Libraries that create unrealistic expectations around perfectionism effectively force minoritized, marginalized, or racialized staff or colleagues to play lead in a role for which they were never prepared.

> **Conversational Prompt (Action): Owning Our Role in the Practice of Perfectionism.**
>
> 1. How might perfectionism adversely impact minoritized, marginalized, or racialized staff in your library?
> 2. How do you set expectations and create a safe space for these staff or colleagues to seek clarity through questions?
> 3. **For minoritized, marginalized, or racialized staff:** In what ways have you noticed perfection in your organization? How has it impacted you? (Please note that you do not have to publicly share your response to this question)
> 4. Professional excellence means different things to different people. When aligned with a shared goal, do you (your organization) welcome varied representations of success?
> 5. Are there aspects of professionalism that should be standardized? What are they?

This chapter doesn't seek to discount the need for professional excellence. After all, setting priorities for organizational goals, and instituting policies and procedures in service of a dynamic patron experience is the lifeblood of what we do. By deepening our understanding of perfectionism, we have greater insight into those moments when we are pushing ourselves and others in ways that may create professional doubt or discomfort. Whether you notice this behavior in yourself or your team, it will be important to address the practice early on. A helpful approach to this is completing an exercise that I call The Perfection Question.

The Perfection Question exercise uses a series of guided questions that invite participants to consider the similarities between perfect and imperfect outcomes with the idea of setting and shaping realistic goals. To engage in this exercise, consider a current practice that may be impacted by perfectionism, and ask the following questions.

1. What is a perfect outcome?
2. What is a good outcome?
3. Are there any similarities between the perfect and good outcomes?

4. Are there glaring differences between the perfect and good outcomes?

5. Is our level of service compromised if the outcome isn't perfect?

6. What is the most ideal path forward?

In completing this exercise, you may discover that your desired outcome doesn't require perfectionism, but rather a better understanding of the needs of both your internal and external community.

It's time for us to acknowledge how the culture of perfectionism shows up in our libraries. Beyond admission, beyond recognition, an organizational approach to shifting the focus from always perfect to always present starts with these steps. Step 1: Begin to normalize conversations about mistakes and talk about how they can be harnessed and operationalized for growth. Step 2: Be open about your organizational pain points related to perfectionism; the more you're able to acknowledge when and why perfectionism is prioritized, the easier it is to counteract the behaviors. Step 3: Recognize that perfectionism isn't the singular trait of an accomplished organization. Other than the polished perception of your library, what sets you apart, what makes you unique, how are you acting in service to your patrons, and most importantly, what makes people want to come to the library? Step 4: Imagine: What might a new approach to professional standards look like for your organization? Who is invited to the table to share their ideas? You now have an opportunity to include participants whose ideas and perspectives were never considered.

Yes, we are working in service of positive perception. We want our community to know and love us. And, we do want to get things right. But getting it right for our communities is meeting them where they are, being responsive to their needs, and showing up each day as who we are. I'm almost positive that it has very little to do with staff, collections, spaces, services, or facilities being perfect.

3 All the Write Words

White Supremacy Work Culture Characteristic: Worship the Written Word

> **Warning Signs for Worship of the Word**
> - Micromanaging internal communications
> - Not allowing colleagues time to process information
> - Document overload
> - Weaponizing our written policies

When it comes to the aspects of white supremacy work culture, worship of the written word is often one of the tenets of work culture behaviors that give library workers pause. After all, our very existence centers on the written word and language. As we continue to unpack the influences of White Supremacy Work Culture on librarianship, we do so not to diminish the role of libraries as places that center literacy and learning, but rather to encourage a deeper and more introspective analysis of the degree to which the written word is used both internally and mechanized externally to create environments in which those who have a greater understanding of the constructs of language (for a variety of reasons) thrive and how those who are not linguistically gifted may find the workplace challenging.

Quite simply, the concept of worship of the written word is the policing of the language used within or in reference to the library. If one were to see the descriptor for this white supremacy work culture tenet, they may falsely believe that the practice of worship of the written word simply explains the "red pen" revising and editing, or excessive Google doc commenting of a person committed to effective communication. However, worship of the written word isn't a mere commitment to standardizing language or modeling consistency.

There is a built-in inequity in the practice of worship of the written word as it places value not on the message itself, but rather on the messenger. It is a behavior that is designed to reinforce the choices we make about how much we will (or won't) value the perspectives of the person speaking.

Worship of the written word may look like:

- [ ] An inability to see beyond written policy and procedure.
- [ ] Considering the written word as the only means of sharing knowledge or ideas.
- [ ] Amplifying or **tokenizing** those who can communicate well through written words.
- [ ] Creating a sense of inadequacy for those for whom the written word isn't a strength.

Each of these behaviors affects internal structures and relationships. In fact, worship of the written word is often one of the most insidious tactics used to create internal hierarchy. Those who are considered highly effective written communicators may often find themselves asked to draft or edit documents, adding to their workflow and creating in them a sense of frustration and fatigue. Colleagues who may learn or interpret information more effectively through visual, aural, or auditory methods may find themselves excluded from idea generation or decision-making opportunities. In instances where individuals feel judged or marginalized due to their communication practices or abilities, there is also a collective sense of fear and reticence to develop or share ideas.

Perhaps the greatest risk of worship of the written word is its tendency to create a workplace culture where written documentation is the singular form of respected communication. In libraries, the tunnel vision created by our desire to focus solely on the written word shows up in policy and procedure development, often creating a service vacuum, particularly when there is an immediacy of need. Yes, the written word in the form of policy and procedure provides us with a professional roadmap and a collective sense of understanding that everyone in the organization shares.

But is there an opportunity within the scope of our commitment to policy and procedure to create space for unscripted actions and behaviors that allow us to galvanize the community and meet the ever-changing needs of the people we serve? What might it look like to have levity beyond what is written? How might a departure from the written word inspire new opportunities for organizational growth and communication?

Beyond policy and procedure, worship of the written word may also show up in our internal communications. Have you noted unspoken expectations around email response times within your organization? Do colleagues send emails or texts related to work after working hours? It is important to note that worship of the written word not only includes the written word, but also an approach to communication that demands that the information shared is prioritized.

Consider, for a moment, the internal culture of communication in your organization. Building an awareness around the behaviors we exhibit that promote and encourage worship of the written word requires us to practice the discomfort of honest reflection. This awareness demands that we interrogate the behaviors (both organizational and personal) that have led to the centering of worship of the written word.

Conversational Prompt (Awareness): Written Word and Your Organization

1. What unspoken rules or parameters exist in my organizational communication?
2. When correspondence that requires a response is shared, are staff given enough time to read, interpret, and respond?
3. Is document overload a trait of our organization?
4. How might my organization be creating fear or reticence around written communication?
5. How might I be experiencing fear or reticence related to communication?
6. In what ways have we created a culture where those who are strong written communicators are favored, and those who aren't are not?

As a child, my mom would often chastise me about my messy room. One of her favorite points of connection for getting me to consider the impact of my personal mess was to ask how I would feel if my friends or teacher saw my room. Interestingly, the invitation for me to consider the impact that my messy room could have on valued relationships always provided me with the impetus to clean. What my mom recognized was that I cared about the opinions and reactions of my friends and teachers, and finding a point of connection with the thing that I valued most made all the difference.

Behaviors associated with worship of the written word in our libraries are our "messy room." We know there is an existing problem with the ways we communicate; we may even acknowledge openly that the problem exists, but unless we are challenged to consider how our misuse and centering of the written word may have negative impacts, we stop short of addressing the problem. And the root cause of this mess is not hidden socks and shoes, but rather hidden agendas that are created through the ways in which we communicate and invite communication. What is your point of connection with the community you serve? When challenged to consider how valued relationships may be impacted by an organization's reliance on the written word, do you have the impetus to move?

We demonstrate our commitment to decentering written words by recognizing that there are many other ways of inviting authentic community feedback. Beyond surveys or stakeholder interviews, the shift from the worship of the written word requires us to engage in more organic methodologies for storytelling and story gathering. Examples of this include talking circles, group forums, or recorded perspectives—methods that shift the focus from writing to practices that more authentically measure the patron experience.

Demonstrating a commitment to creating space for community stories starts with the understanding that conveying thought or opinion shouldn't be limited solely to the written word, and that expression of feeling can be done through a variety of inclusive mediums. The result of cultivating this understanding establishes libraries as places that value the stories of our patrons, even if their stories or perspectives don't positively support our current practices. For example, a community member may share that they don't feel children's library staff are engaged and connected with the families they serve, but enjoy the wide array of children's programming offered. Rather than taking into consideration the feedback on staff, worship of the written word creates in us a fear of acknowledging those aspects of library services that we can improve upon. Instead, we focus solely on the positive "we enjoy library programming." This is a dangerous practice because this behavior doesn't provide an honest reflection of community sentiment around the library, and it doesn't challenge the library to be more evaluative of important issues, like staff engagement.

Understanding the fear inspired by the worship of the written word helps us to develop a professional vulnerability that gently nudges us to move beyond fixed mindsets. There are many ways that the worship of the written word may impact your community engagement. Be mindful of instances when you:

- ☐ Take only the parts and pieces of a story that strengthen the library's message.
- ☐ Censor comments or feedback to remove negative sentiments.
- ☐ Volunteer to assist community partners in "drafting" language to reflect their relationships with the library.
- ☐ Question or challenge methods of communication used by marginalized groups before establishing context or working toward relationship-building.

Yes, even in libraries, there can be a lack of understanding and listening to stories. And, just as with my impetus to clean my messy room, libraries must do the work of acknowledging both the tremendous value of our communities and how failing to address our tendencies toward worship of the written word may act as a limiter, preventing us from fully leaning into a community-building purpose.

> **Conversational Prompt (Accountability): The Part We Play in Worship of the Written Word**
>
> 1. Other than written communication, what methods have you used to engage with the community?
> 2. Do our behaviors around communication and language exhibit an authentic desire to connect with and listen to our patrons?
> 3. What might you do to shift organizational behaviors around stories and storytelling to be more inclusive?
> 4. In what ways does worship of the written word show up in your library? Emails? Planning documents? Policy development?

Speaker and author Yahuda Berg famously said, "Words have energy and power with the ability to help, to heal, to hinder, to hurt, to harm, to humiliate, and to humble." Within this context, it becomes clear how worship of the written word both diminishes the positive aspects of language and communication and amplifies its most negative outcomes. With this understanding, how do we harness the power of this information to create better systems of communication for our libraries?

Building understanding of organizational behaviors around communication and language may simply begin through self-reflection. Set aside time to consider your personal relationship with the written word. Sometimes the first step in this process requires you to answer a question: Do you set healthy boundaries for communication? If the answer is yes, that's wonderful; your next step will be to create a list of the ways in which you practice healthy communication. If your answer is no, then it will be important for you to take the time needed to reflect upon the ways in which worship of the written word shows up and informs your working relationships.

It is important to understand that while you may be responding to the behaviors of worship of the written word, you may not be the person initiating these behaviors. A great question to help you determine your "role" in worship of the written word behavior is to ask yourself—Am I the person sending after-hours work emails or texts? Or am I the person who is choosing to respond to them?

The next step in this process is to take a broad view of organizational behaviors related to the worship of the written word. As a department or team, you may want to develop a systems-level knowledge of the written documentation in your organization and how this language may be used or misused. An example of this would be to consider the often ambiguous nature of library policies. Review your own, and consider those who may be directly or indirectly affected by them.

Do you find that duality exists in your policies, noting that in one instance, a policy may be used to trespass a patron, and in another instance, with a different patron, the same policy may be overlooked or ignored? As you take a deep dive into your analysis of documents, this is also an opportunity to consider the ways in which we favor the written word over ingenuity and creativity. Think of the library worker who is admonished because they deviate from a departmental manual to try something new.

This systems-level review of documentation may encourage opportunities for challenging conversations around the expectations set by library leadership. Consider the manager who actively commits microaggressions and macroaggressions through internal communications platforms when they are unhappy with perceived inefficiencies. Taking the time to conduct both individual and organizational reflection will illuminate the many ways that the written word can be weaponized in our libraries. Use the conversational prompts below to support you in beginning this process.

> **Conversational Prompt (Action): Re-centering Our Approach to Communication**
> 1. Consider your library policies. Can you find instances of ambiguity?
> 2. What, if any, role might you play in creating an internal culture that promotes worship of the written word? What steps might you take to shift this narrative?
> 3. What does transforming behaviors that center worship of the written word look like for you?
> 4. Do worship of the written word behaviors exist on our team? What steps might we take to acknowledge this behavior?

I could tell you that transforming behaviors associated with worship of the written word is an easy and seamless process, but that wouldn't be true. But I will tell you that it starts with YOU. I encourage you to take the time to think about your relationship with the written word. What might a shift in our approach to the written word do for our internal and external communities? We do have the power to transform the insistence of impossible rules and behaviors around language and communication, but before we can make these changes, we must recognize the need for them.

4 No Time to Spare

White Supremacy Work Culture Characteristic: Sense of Urgency

> **Warning Signs for Sense of Urgency**
> - Personal/Professional burnout
> - Having to restart, reset, or renew
> - Process over people mentality
> - Not prioritizing the time needed to cultivate meaningful relationships or have meaningful conversations.

Everywhere you go people are hurrying toward something. It could be that person tailgating you on the highway, or the person behind you in the grocery line, quietly drumming their fingers as you question the price of a scanned item; it feels like the people around us are creating the rules for how quickly we move through life, and we are powerless to stop it. This idea of denying one's agency, careful decision-making, and perspective in favor of moving quickly toward the completion of a task or goal is a white supremacy work culture behavior known as a sense of urgency. It is easy to recognize daily patterns that are demonstrative of a sense of urgency—people who are impatient, family members who prioritize their own needs over your own. But, are we able to recognize a sense of urgency in our work environments? Do we recognize the impatience that exists in our organizations? Have we normalized these behaviors, making a sense of urgency an expected call to action that we use to both set expectations for others and ourselves?

When a sense of urgency becomes customary practice in our organizations, it is often conflated with driving innovation, inspiring change, or taking performance to the next level. If performance were the singular rubric by which we measured success, then one might believe that a sense of urgency was a dynamic model for inspiring organizational change. At best, a sense of urgency increases staff productivity and may drive the faster completion of assignments and projects. The expectation created by a sense of urgency may also inspire staff to take on more to be seen as valued contributors to the team. At worst, a sense of urgency creates fissures in a collaborative working environment, making staff fearful of expressing feelings of anxiety, stress, or fatigue. It's also important to note that just as a sense of urgency can be created by others and imposed on us, there is also an internalized sense of urgency that we may create for ourselves, a personal mandate that requires us to do more, work more, and accomplish more. When it shows up in our working spaces, it looks like:

- [ ] Constantly feeling like you're in flux or don't have enough time.
- [ ] Setting unrealistic timelines and expectations for internal projects.
- [ ] Creating a correlation between the amount of time it takes for someone to complete a project and their professional abilities.
- [ ] Decision-making structures that don't encourage or allow for varied perspectives.

In libraries, a sense of urgency can happen at various stages in our careers. We recognize this behavior in early career librarians who bridge organizational participation and professional engagement on a local, state, or national level, taking advantage of every growth opportunity. We see this behavior in mid-career librarians who are engaging in the often-exhausting work of managing teams and leading projects in preparation for a big professional leap. We also see this sense of urgency in library workers who, after many years, have made the decision to pursue their MLIS and are preparing for their futures by taking on added roles and responsibilities. It doesn't matter whether the sense of urgency is welcomed or not; the demands that come with a culture of proving our worth through work almost always cause a critical case of imbalance.

Recognition and awareness are powerful tools in addressing an organizational culture rooted in a sense of urgency. Consider your internal culture and its behaviors: Are they informed by long-held institutional knowledge? One of the most pervasive ways that a sense of urgency is created in our libraries is through meetings. Often required, meetings create a built-in expectation and sense of urgency for both the person leading the meeting and the individuals attending.

You don't have to be the person planning a meeting to begin thinking about the sense of urgency that meetings create. Start by thinking about your organizational approach to meetings. When you consider your organizational goals, do you find that meetings are prioritized over doing? Are expectations set around the length or frequency of meetings? How might a culture of meetings be affecting you, your team, or your organization? You may discover that meetings are the foundation upon which behaviors centering a sense of urgency are built.

> **Conversational Prompt: Awareness**
>
> 1. When was the first time that you realized you weren't working at your own pace?
> 2. What is your approach to completing other duties as assigned?
> 3. In what ways does your organization create a sense of urgency?
> 4. How do you respond when someone creates a sense of urgency for you?
> 5. In what ways might you be creating a sense of urgency for those around you?
> 6. When was the last time that you (your organization) evaluated your approach to meetings?

Maxine Waters famously popularized the phrase "reclaiming my time." This idea of reclamation of time eloquently sums up the effects that an unchecked sense of urgency can have on our working lives. In fact, one of the primary traits of a sense of urgency is feeling as if you never have enough time to get things done. For many of us, we understand this trait all too well. Even as you feel you have everything for your day mapped out and organized, there always seems to be a new responsibility, problem to solve, or question to answer. But sadly, an increased demand on our schedules doesn't come with more hours being added to the day or cleared spaces on our calendars. In libraries, the transparency around a created sense of urgency is even built into the ways we write our job postings. How many of you are familiar with this sentence: "Candidate will also complete other duties as assigned." While we may not realize it, the use of these words sets an expectation for overwork and overwhelm. They create an often-untenable work environment that mandates that, from day one, we take on every unclaimed or unwanted responsibility, all to ensure the greater good of the library.

Now, let's be clear. Someone must do the work, and chances are . . . it's all of us. However, it is important for libraries and library workers (I'm looking at you, library leaders) to examine our roles in contributing to the **mission fatigue** that is pervasive in our profession. According to a recent study conducted by **Microsoft**, more than 50 percent of workers across the world experience burnout. How are we in our libraries contributing to these alarming numbers? We must ask ourselves if what we gain through the Pavlovian-like responses to creating a sense of urgency in our libraries is worth the long-term risks of creating an unhappy work culture. What might it look like to remove phrases like "other duties as assigned" from our applications? I'm willing to guess that the applicant will readily join your team prepared to do their jobs, even without its inclusion.

> **Conversational Prompt: Accountability**
> 1. In a perfect world, what might "reclaiming your time" look like for you?
> 2. How does your organization create psychological safety for staff to express concerns about behaviors that promote a sense of urgency?
> 3. Does your current job application include the phrase "other duties as assigned." How might you convey the varying roles and responsibilities of a position without using this language?
> 4. What happens when timelines aren't met? How might you work to create a better system of setting and meeting project milestones?

In our libraries, a sense of urgency shows up in many different ways. Addressing these behaviors requires four steps: (1) that we respond to the behavior in the moment, (2) be prepared to detail why the behavior creates a sense of urgency, (3) that we can clearly demonstrate through example the impacts of the behavior, and (4) that we come prepared to present an alternative.

Here's an example of what this may look like:

Step 1: Carol, I'm concerned because you've changed the timeline for our project three times. Each time, the timeline has been abbreviated.

Step 2: When you make these changes without inviting the perspectives of the team, it doesn't consider our individual schedules or projects, and it creates a sense of urgency for each of us.

Step 3: For example, I now have two major deadlines due on the same day.

Step 4: Would it be possible for us to come together to discuss a shift to the timeline that will honor your desire to abbreviate the schedule while working with us to identify potential scheduling conflicts?

A sense of urgency is absolute in creating stress for the person on the receiving end of the behavior; you may find that the most frequent "culprit" has no idea that they are the person responsible. If the person leading the charge on creating a sense of urgency holds a position of power or is blissfully unchanged after being made aware of their culpability in promoting this behavior, the rules of engagement needed to address these concerns may require you to choose your own adventure. In other words, employ a different strategy—a strategy that requires you to set and feel safe in prioritizing boundaries for your own professional well-being. You don't have to share these boundaries with anyone, simply know them for yourself and remain committed to holding true to them. Recognizing a sense of urgency in others and ourselves can be difficult. Whether a person recognizes their role in engaging in this behavior, or not, here you'll find a list of the most pervasive behaviors informed by a sense of urgency in the workplace.

- Colleagues not meeting their personal deadlines and creating added work for you to meet their goals.
- Sharing an exciting new opportunity with a member of your staff, and not giving them time to process whether or not the opportunity is best for them.

- Setting unrealistic expectations for yourself as a means of building professional or personal momentum.
- Driving the completion of large projects through withholding behaviors (denying vacations, mandating weekend work, requiring additional hours or effort)
- Introducing departmental processes for staff without considering the inclusivity of your implementation practices.

How many of these examples felt familiar to you? Let's talk about how you can begin to take the actions needed to address a sense of urgency in your organization.

> **Conversational Prompt: Action**
> 1. Consider the sense of urgency in your organization. What must change?
> 2. How comfortable are you in addressing a sense of urgency in the moment? What might make you feel more empowered to speak up?
> 3. What steps might you take if the person creating the sense of urgency in your organization is in a position of power?
> 4. Create a list of personal boundaries to prevent a sense of urgency. **Note:** You do not have to share your list.

To ensure that you understand how a sense of urgency shows up in the workplace, let's work through a few scenarios. I don't know about you, but scenarios really help me unpack what I learn, and I hope that they will do the same for you. While these scenarios may be completed individually, you may find that they present an opportunity for engaging in robust conversation and idea sharing. Most importantly, the responses should not be analyzed for correctness or incorrectness, and you shouldn't get distracted by right or wrong responses. As with most things, there will be varied perspectives. While I have provided "answers" to the questions following each scenario (**answers can be found in the Appendix**), my responses are not an exhaustive list. I encourage you to both formulate your own responses and consider the ways in which the examples are demonstrative of your individual behaviors and those of your team or organization.

Scenario 1: My Problem Is Your Problem

Dr. Jenn Fowler, a tenured member of the Music Department faculty, often uses library resources. She often uses the library to prepare for auditions, including researching music compositions, making copies, and laminating. More than once, Dr. Fowler has shown up at the library ten minutes before class to make copies. Feeling rushed, she often asks that library staff make copies and bring them to her class. Most recently, she visited the library to laminate a large-scale project and was disappointed to learn that the laminating machine takes fifteen minutes to warm up. Frustrated, she said, "I have class in five minutes. Will someone on staff laminate and cut these for me, I'll have a student come to pick them up."

1. Awareness: Is Dr. Fowler creating a sense of urgency?
2. Accountability: Who is affected by Dr. Fowler's behaviors?
3. Accountability: Who might feel disempowered to address this sense of urgency?
4. Action: How might you address Dr. Fowler?

Scenario 2: The Rush to the Finish Line

Recently, you were asked to act as project manager for a community partnership that would provide Wi-Fi to an underserved community. While there is no race to the finish line for the project, you understand that only two libraries, including your own, have been given the opportunity to pilot this innovative program. The project provides you with an abundance of resources, including the time necessary to assemble a working committee with library staff from across the city. Of course, it would be fantastic to gain the perspectives of colleagues, particularly those who work at the branch that serves the community who will be receiving the free Wi-Fi. But imagine the positive press for the library if you were to pilot the program first. Instead of creating a working committee, you decide to assemble a small group of trusted fellow administrators who work with you at the Main Library. They represent a cross-section of departments and should be able to support you in efficiently and effectively hastening the process.

1. Awareness: In what ways do you note a sense of urgency?
2. Awareness: Who might be affected by this sense of urgency?
3. Action: What might the library staff at the community branch do to ensure that they aren't excluded or silenced during this process?

Scenario 3: I'm Growing and Tired

Khari, an early career librarian, hasn't stopped since their first year as a librarian. They currently serve on two internal committees, plan all adult programming for their location, and have recently become active with their state's library association. While they have loved their library work and have enjoyed the connections made through their community of practice, Khari is fearful of taking on added responsibilities. In fact, they are unsure of how much longer they will be able to successfully complete tasks. In spite of this, when asked to join a committee tasked with planning summer programming, they enthusiastically agree.

1. Awareness: How is a sense of urgency showing up in this scenario?
2. Accountability: Who is creating the sense of urgency? Khari? The library?
3. Awareness: What emotions or feelings are you sensing in Khari? Action: How might they continue a trajectory of success while addressing the sense of urgency?
4. Action: How might Khari's manager be more mindful of fostering a sense of urgency for the staff?

So, how did you enjoy the scenarios? I hope that you were able to use the "problems" posed in the scenarios to find real-time solutions for your library. There is no denying that a sense of urgency exists in our libraries. This white supremacy work culture trait perfectly aligns with the concept of **vocational awe** that we often experience as library workers. As Fobazi Ettarh, who developed this concept, says, "A healthy workplace is one where working around the clock is not seen as a requirement."

This means that we don't have to allow a sense of urgency to inform our ideas of success or failure as library workers. It's time that we recognize that faster doesn't necessarily mean better. We do this by encouraging library workers to practice with intentionality that shows the complexity and agility required of our roles. But, most importantly, we leave behind the "other duties as assigned" culture that prepares individuals joining LIS professions for the predestined sense of urgency that comes with a work environment that prioritizes giving more work over giving more time.

5 The Way It's Always Been Done

White Supremacy Work Culture Characteristic: One Right Way

> **Warning Signs for One Right Way**
> - Internal fear of failure
> - Non-individualized Thinking
> - Fixed Mindsets

One of my most memorable experiences as a librarian was when I started my first job at a public library. As is customary in many public libraries, there is a tremendous amount of excitement and planning that goes into organizing the Summer Reading program. And, a big part of the excitement for library staff is the unveiling and distribution of branded Summer Reading T-shirts (side note: I think we can agree that they are the most comfortable shirts ever made). Being new to my role, I decided to wear my new T-shirt on one of the designated "casual Fridays." That Friday, as I confidently proceeded to my office, I was stopped in my tracks by a colleague I'd never met. "Excuse me," she said, "you're not supposed to have that shirt on." Perplexed, I panicked, "isn't this casual Friday?" I asked. "Am I not able to wear T-shirts?" "T-shirts are fine," she corrected, "you're just not supposed to wear a Summer Reading T-shirt until the official start of Summer Reading." "Oh . . . okay, is this posted anywhere?" I asked, feeling embarrassed. "No," she replied, "it's just the way it's always worked."

What I didn't know then, and recognize now, is that this was an example of the white supremacy work culture tenet known as One Right Way. In libraries, One Right Way characteristics are often recognized as institutional knowledge or internal practice. They are the systematic ways of being and doing in our organizations, the ways both large and small, that we enforce unwritten behavioral standards. Unlike worship of the written Word and its reliance on those policies or procedures that are written, the actions and reactions inspired by One Right Way behaviors are often born of a singular idea or perspective that is shared from one person to another, until it becomes an unspoken behavioral standard. And, in the example that I shared with you, the unspoken behavioral standard in my library was waiting until summer reading officially began before wearing a T-shirt. Remember, I shared with you that One Right Way behaviors show up in both large and small ways. And, my T-shirt faux pas was one of these "small" instances. There was nothing terribly wrong about my colleagues' behavior, she only sought to inform me of something I didn't know. I, however, was caught unaware, surprised to learn that in addition to everything else I'd need to learn as an early career librarian, I'd also need to figure out all of the unwritten rules that existed in my organization. Beyond corrections over T-shirts, break room etiquette, or celebration norms, there exist many other more insidious ways that One Right Way thinking shows up in our organizations.

Although anyone can demonstrate One Right Way behaviors, in its most damaging form, it is leveraged by those who hold positions of power. Fearing the uncertainty that comes with change, library leaders who hold fast to One Right Way thinking limit themselves and others in the pursuit of maintaining the status quo. Imagine the circulation manager who is so singularly committed to a long-held library card sign-up process that they are unwilling to entertain feedback on a small change that may break existing barriers to access that currently exist. Or, perhaps One Right Way thinking and internal culture have become so interconnected that any attempts at introducing new ideas, perspectives, or methods related to shifting approach are seen by those in leadership as perceived threats instead of opportunities.

When put into practice, One Right Way behaviors become evident in the form of extreme checks and balances, disinterest in new ideas, and fear of disruption or change. It also exists in our organizational lexicon through the use of language like "this method is best practice," "this is the way it's always been done," or "don't try that, it won't work." And while One Right Way methodologies are rarely attached to formalized organizational policies that are more widely known, they still have the power to shape our organizations by informing the internal actions of library workers, making them fearful of coloring outside of the lines or trying anything new. In organizations where One Right Way behaviors go unnoticed or unaddressed, there exists a clear disregard for the many varied strengths, backgrounds, abilities, and lived experiences of their internal community. Other demonstrations of this disregard include:

- [ ] Internal processes are rooted in a singular best practice.
- [ ] Taking a "because I said so" approach to questions or suggestions that may require change.
- [ ] Discomfort in pivoting, being agile in the workplace, or making compromises on the fly.
- [ ] Discouraging or reprimanding staff from trying something new.
- [ ] Engaging in outreach efforts from a place of superiority.

For those of you reading who gain greater clarity when you're able to create a throughline between the idea you're currently learning and a similar concept, I'd like to share with you how the idea of One Right Way thinking has reverberations beyond white supremacy work culture. In her book *Mindset*, American psychologist Carol Dweck details two approaches to thinking and learning that she calls mindsets. According to Dweck, a fixed mindset approach centers an apprehension of those things that are new or different. Conversely, she believes, a growth mindset is rooted in a willingness to try, even if trying creates discomfort.

Quite simply, in our libraries, One Right Way approaches are fixed mindset approaches; they are solidly rooted in an "if it ain't broke, don't fix it" mentality. And, just as fixed, One Right Way behaviors thrive on stasis; the momentum needed to shift our organizational and individual practices to reflect growth mindset behaviors will require us to acknowledge and address our fear responses related to change.

> **Conversational Prompt: Awareness**
> 1. In what ways have you noted One Right Way thinking in your library?
> 2. How might you address the reticence to invite or acknowledge new ideas?
> 3. When was the last time you or your team tried a new practice or procedure? Was it successful? How did you manage the challenges?

To operationalize and optimize behaviors that are counter to One Right Way thinking, we start by questioning why we allow certain systems in our libraries to persist. What might we gain from an openness to change? Why is a process precious to our organization or team? We grow our fearlessness by challenging ourselves to view the process of questioning as an invitation to explore what it might look like to try a new approach. This new approach may look like a renewed commitment to leaning into the discomfort of change.

It may also include reevaluating how we allow colleagues who place a weighted value on uniformity or sameness to hold space or drive false narratives around what is or isn't a healthy, collaborative work culture. To address instances where colleagues may find it difficult to consider ideas or beliefs that are counter to One Right Way thinking, we can:

1. **Acknowledge feelings and perspectives.**
   Purpose: To create a psychologically safe platform where a person can share concerns.
2. **Invite individuals to share the significance of a "precious" practice and why it resonates so deeply.**
   Purpose: To better understand the basis for their actions or reactions related to the practice.
3. **Ask them to consider both the positive and negative impacts of the current practice and of the proposed change.**
   Purpose: To encourage communication about varied perspectives and alleviate associated fears or anxieties.

Note: You may find that the individual will identify far more negative impacts for a proposed change than positive impacts. But in asking these questions, you invite them to begin thinking about the process of change.

4. **Address Behaviors**

   Purpose: To establish awareness of an existing behavior and to make clear the associated outcomes and implications.

   While it often feels easier to accept or ignore One Right Way behaviors, these four steps demonstrate what it could look like to take intentional and proactive approaches to reshaping internal culture.

Conversational Prompt: Accountability

1. In what ways is asking questions to examine a process or procedure encouraged? Discouraged?
2. What are the "precious" processes or procedures in your organization? How might they benefit from new ideas or approaches?
3. In what ways is your organization fearful of change? How might you address this?

Transforming organizational culture around One Right Way thinking also requires libraries to consider the value add of library workers who are up for the challenge of doing things differently. Many years ago, I had an opportunity to take an improv for leaders class at The Second City, a renowned comedy club, theater, and school of improvisation. During the class, the instructors shared with us an exercise that they called Yes, And. Partnered in groups of two, the purpose of this exercise was to keep the conversation going by responding to each comment made by your exercise partner by responding, Yes, And—contributing additional details to strengthen the original idea.

Full disclosure, my partner and I quickly accepted the challenge—elevating our imagined library program into a star-studded event with performances from Beyonce and Bon Jovi. And, as I continued to add to my partner's big ideas, I quickly realized that with every Yes, And, we gave each other permission to be creative and take risks that would otherwise have felt ridiculous. I think that this was the point the instructors were trying to make. While it felt quite counterintuitive to begin, it only took a few moments to fully realize our potential for creative thinking. How might you operationalize the idea of Yes, And with your teams or colleagues to begin breaking down the barriers to innovation created by One Right Way approaches?

The concept of Yes, And may also be used to evaluate internal service models that aren't as agile and flexible as they should be. A crucial characteristic of One Right Way thinking is an approach to partnership development and community building that is often informed through a lens of superiority, with libraries holding greater power and priority than partnering organizations. A re-envisioning of our engagement with partners through the use of Yes, And might start with an idea: **We will transform our approach to partnership development.** While every idea won't necessarily be successful, the sharing of multiple good ideas often leads to the development of one great idea born of innovation.

Conversational Prompt: Action

1. How might you use a "yes, and" approach to transforming One Right Way behaviors in your organization? Your team?

2. What might you (your organization, your team) do to become more comfortable with compromise or change?

3. How might you operationalize the idea of Yes, And in your organization?

4. Transforming our One Right Way-focused behaviors will require us to_____.

> **Yes, And—an Example**
>
> **Instructions:** Break into partnered groups of two. Ask the first person who speaks to share a big idea related to your team. The second person is asked to build on the first idea by responding Yes, And then following up with their own big idea that will support the original concept. As long as the great ideas are flowing, let the back and forth between partners continue.
>
> **Example:**
>
> **First Person:** Let's begin addressing the ways in which One Right Way approaches are impacting our internal culture.
>
> **Second Person:** Yes, and this shift will inform library workers who are able to creatively address and remedy problems, and understand how to apply a nuanced approach to problem-solving.
>
> **First Person:** Yes, and in addition to this shift informing library workers who are able to creatively address and remedy problems, and understand how to apply a nuanced approach to problem-solving. We also signal that we are open to change and recognize the value of different ideas and perspectives.

The fixed nature of library policies, procedures, services, and supports naturally creates environments where One Right Way behaviors thrive. We recognize that our service models are built on uniformity because we serve everyone. We believe that it's safer to hold on to certain processes because we know they work. And, how many of us know all too well how the idea of making change-related choices that may inform or transform how our libraries are seen, respected, or valued can inspire tremendous fear?

And that's just it. . . . One Right Way thinking in our organizations is functioning at its best when we are persistently driven to decision or indecision by fear. How do we serve our ever-evolving communities if we're afraid to introduce or adapt to change? How do we champion community needs when we are afraid to assess and reassess our own? And, most importantly, how do we invite the sharing of community perspectives and ideas if we don't value the perspectives and ideas of our staff, colleagues, or teams?

PART 2

A Practice in Reflection

By now, I hope that you are finding ways to engage in reflection (self or group) around the white supremacy work culture tenets that you've learned. As you engage in this reflection, take note of both your individual accountability, awareness, and action related to white supremacy work culture behaviors, and the larger collective responses of your team to engage in the practice of accountability, awareness, and action. You may find that while you are willing to do the work of examining your individual role in championing or playing a part in certain White Supremacy Work Culture behaviors, your team, colleagues, or even library leaders are not.

And while you are clearly able to find alignment between the behaviors shown in your working environment and the white supremacy work culture tenets, you may discover that your colleagues, team, or library leadership are unable, unwilling, or unprepared to do the same. If this is the case for you, then take this journey of discovery for yourself, applying what you've learned to engage in your own grassroots efforts to transform White Supremacy Work Culture in your organization. If you and your team have been able to engage in authentic discussions about the current state of your working environment, I encourage you to continue challenging what you think you know about your organization.

But, as with most things, it is the willingness with which we approach our accountability and awareness of behaviors that will inform our future actions—actions that decide whether we will continue operationalizing organizational norms like perfectionism, worship of the written word, a sense of urgency, and One Right Way thinking. It is important that we consider how and why we've allowed these behaviors to become normalized in our organizations. Who has benefited from these behaviors? Who hasn't benefited? And in doing this, we should also consider what it might look like to eliminate "normalized" behaviors that don't invite expression of identity, value dimensions of diversity, or welcome varied insights or methodologies.

Working in pursuit of what could be rather than what is or was will require us to deeply consider what we will carry over into the next iteration of our organizational identities. Before beginning Part 2 of the book, let's take a moment to consider what you've discovered so far.

WSWC Part 1 Introspection

1. The behavioral norm-based White Supremacy Work Culture Behavior that is most present in my organization is (perfectionism, worship of the written word, a sense of urgency, and One Right Way thinking).
2. We are ready to do the work of addressing this behavior because . . .
3. We aren't ready to address this behavior because . . .
4. Addressing this behavior will require that I/we do the following.
5. Not addressing this behavior will . . .
6. Successfully addressing this behavior will . . .

Thoughtfully considering the conversational prompts shared in each chapter along with the introspective reflection questions shared above will support you in shaping a framework for the next steps needed to fully interrogate White Supremacy Work Culture behavioral norms that exist in your organization. In addition to the foundational knowledge gained through the process of asking questions and seeking answers, reshaping our organizational approaches and their intersectionality with White Supremacy Work Culture will require us to change the internal behaviors that we have allowed to thrive in our organizations. This comes with the acknowledgment that while we may not have planted the seeds of White Supremacy Work Culture, in many ways our acquiescence to and acceptance of these behaviors have contributed to their growth in our working environments.

The power to shift our organizational culture comes from our understanding of what White Supremacy Work Culture behaviors are and how they show up. After all, how can we solve a problem that we don't know exists? I have a colleague who often says, "let's just call a thing, a thing." In other words, let's not be fearful of addressing a problem. Our ability to build skill in addressing the problem of white supremacy work culture is vital in supporting our forward trajectory. It is the recognition that while a project may not have been a success, this doesn't mean that the person leading that project isn't successful. Or understanding that failure isn't inherently negative and could act as a catalyst for positive change.

For some, addressing the problem of white supremacy work culture may require the consideration of how worship of the written word is affecting internal culture and creating deeper issues around power, privilege, and equity. For others, it may require the development of a plan for how they will effectively make decisions in environments where urgency is the conditioned response. In addressing the problem of white supremacy work culture, we can (and should) create space to identify and acknowledge the different paths and approaches to the shared goal of moving beyond perfectionism, worship of the written word, sense of urgency, and One Right Way thinking.

As we begin Part 2 of the book, I encourage you to consider the behaviors that we've learned so far and how they are interconnected, or different.

6   The Myth of Professionalism

Now that you have a better understanding of White Supremacy Work Culture norms in our organizations, we will begin addressing the myth of professionalism. I often refer to professionalism as a "myth" because although the attitudes and behaviors encouraged by professionalism are widely known and accepted, the idea that there is one ideal of being "professional" is a falsehood. Far too often, acting, being, or appearing professional may mean mirroring the behaviors of the dominant group. In our libraries, this cosplayed professionalism can strip library workers of parts of their identity or require the kind of sameness that makes authentic diversity initiatives an impossible dream.

Many of us have been taught that there are certain standards of professionalism that exist in our working environments. As a refresher, I want to share a few professional standards that I've been taught along the way. Are any of these familiar to you?

☐ Go the extra mile.
☐ Keep your work area tidy.
☐ Don't question authority.
☐ Dress for success.

Set a Good Example

Just as I've shared this list of professional standards with you, I'm sure that you can think of many other examples. What are some long-held notions around professionalism that you've been taught? It's also important to note that just as there are many "spoken" practices of professionalism, there also exist many more unspoken practices. For minoritized, marginalized, or racialized library workers, these unspoken standards of professionalism may cause undue harm.

In our libraries, this may show up as:

- [ ] Implicit or explicit biases and microaggressions related to hair or hairstyle.
- [ ] Questioning or invalidating customs or traditions.
- [ ] Creating inequitable standards of communication.
- [ ] Challenging or making light of personal style choices.
- [ ] Introducing meeting formats that prevent staff or colleagues from fully participating.

Acknowledging the mythos behind the practice of professionalism requires us to interrogate what we've been taught about our pathways to success as library workers. As an early career librarian, I was taught that a mark of professionalism was saying "yes" to every opportunity. Over time, I learned that while the opportunities to take part and engage in library work were vast, my resounding yes to every request was creating burnout, underlying frustration, and a skewed work-life balance in me.

Holding on so tightly to what I'd been taught about professionalism, I continued to add to an already full professional plate until I could no longer carry the "weight" of my proverbial plate. Today, many years later, I couldn't even tell you who suggested that I say "yes" to every opportunity. But I can tell you that the impact of that learned professional standard created years of overwhelm for me. What professionalism myths have you been told? What professional myths might you be imparting?

One of the best ways to begin interrogating standards of professionalism is to consider their very existence. In doing this, we can establish both why the professional standard has been prioritized and determine methods for its reprioritization. The process for evaluating professional standards requires that we ask:

1. Who introduced this standard?
2. When was the standard first practiced? When was the standard last reviewed or considered?
3. Who do our standards of professionalism currently serve?

4. Do our professional standards cause harm? Are they rooted in bias, racism, or marginalization?
5. Who is included in conversations around professionalism standards?
6. How do we ensure that all voices and perspectives are heard?
7. What might our organization look like if we emphasized standards of professionalism?

To practice using this exercise, consider a professional standard that is familiar to you or your organization. Pay attention to when the standard was first introduced and last reviewed. You may discover that no one on your team or in your library knows when the professional standard was first practiced or last reviewed. If, in completing the questions, you find that the professional standard that you're addressing causes harm, stop answering questions and take the time needed to unpack both the reasons why you and your team find it harmful. Within the scope of this conversation, it will be important to recognize those colleagues or patrons who may be consciously or unconsciously harmed by the professional standard, identifying clear steps for a path forward. While I hope that you will take the time to answer each of the questions or prompts shared throughout the book, it is important that you be guided by what is happening during your discussions. Use them as a foundational tool, a place to start.

The fact is that professional standards have prevented many of us from fully showing up in the workplace. Far too often, the feeling of being singled out or made to feel **othered** because of set professional standards has become familiar to us. As we turn the corner into part two of the book and learn the aspects of white supremacy work culture that are informed by professionalism, you will have the opportunity to begin unpacking the many reasons you or your organization may be continuing to uphold certain professional standards. Recognizing and understanding the "why" associated with these behaviors will help us to actively dismantle efforts that act in service of one-note approaches to being considered professional. In preparation for the upcoming chapters, define for yourself what you believe professionalism to be.

Setting My Own Standards: An Exercise

1. How do I define professionalism?
2. What are my individual standards of professionalism?
3. Is there alignment between my personal and organizational professional standards?
4. In what ways am I able to reflect my own brand of professionalism in my organization?
5. In what ways am I unable to reflect my own brand of professionalism in my organization?

7 No Conflict Please

White Supremacy Work Culture Characteristic: Fear of Conflict

> **Warning Signs for Fear of Conflict**
> - Staff not feeling psychologically safe.
> - Work environments are filled with uncertainty.
> - Low trust
> - Broken feedback loops

Can you remember the first interaction that you had with a difficult patron, or difference of opinion you had with a colleague? For most of us, these interactions are firmly committed to memory. Even as years go by, we may not remember what the patron wore, or how our colleague responded, but memories of the feelings of frustration, uncertainty, or unease remain. Recently, I had a mini-reunion with colleagues who participated with me in an early career leadership opportunity. Enthusiastic about our future in libraries, we were thrilled to have an opportunity to learn as much as we could from the leaders that had given their time to mentor us. As we reminisced about what we'd learned and where our paths had led us, there was one piece of advice that each of us had received: "As leaders you must measure what you say, and how you say it."

On the surface, the idea of measuring what we say and how we say it simply asks that we are thoughtful in our approach to engaging others, weighing carefully both the intent and impact of our words. But beneath the surface, the ideas that we've often been taught about "measuring what we say"—particularly in our library spaces—not only includes the language that we use to convey our thoughts or perspectives but also points directly to a fear-based response to difficult choices, situations, or people. The uncertainty that shapes and informs whether we respond authentically can best be interpreted through the white supremacy work culture tenet called fear of conflict. In libraries, fear of conflict shows up in many ways. For the library worker who is not in a position of power, fear of conflict may be demonstrated through an inability to express concern about a policy change that may have disparate impacts on communities of color. For a library leader, fear of conflict may create a sense of reticence in addressing a staff member who is challenging to work with. In both instances, fear of conflict acts as a silencer, influencing each individual's ability to effectively express concerns.

A greater issue with the practice of fear of conflict in our libraries are the far-reaching implications that a hesitancy to amplify issues creates, both internally and externally. The often-relational nature of library-centric working environments creates just the right microcosm for fear of conflict behaviors. As library workers, we recognize the many fine lines that exist in our working environments—interdepartmentally, cross-departmentally, in relationships with library administrators, and most importantly, in the relationships we build with the communities we serve. With so many daily interactions and the tremendous investments in relationship-building that library workers make each day, the possibilities for conflict or difference of opinion are magnified. Understanding this, fear of conflict for library workers is often seen as synonymous with causing a disruption or damaging a relationship. When we see fear of conflict in our library spaces, it often shows up as:

- ☐ Library leadership (people who hold power) avoids difficult conversations or situational conflict.
- ☐ Silencing staff who raise tough questions.
- ☐ Relying on a culture of being "polite" or "friendly" as a means of preventing people from authentically expressing opinions or being themselves.
- ☐ Not sharing information that may impact an individual or staff with them directly.

Far too often in our professional environments, there is an operationalized consensus that conflict or difference of opinion should be avoided at all costs. In many ways, the behaviors that exist in support of fear of conflict also coexist with the other demonstrated white supremacy work culture tenets that we've discussed throughout the book. In fact, when we've been taught to apply One Right Way thinking at work and conditioned to believe that perfectionism as a practice is integral to professional success, these two behaviors inform and inspire fear of conflict. After all, who wants to be perceived as negative or combative? And unfortunately, this is what we're taught that conflict is. Fear of conflict as a construct is such a natural human response that even young children cover their eyes or turn away when their parents or caregivers gently ask, "why did you do that?"

In libraries, our fear of conflict is often the proverbial elephant in the room. It is the awareness and recognition of a problem that could be solved if we felt certain that we wouldn't be the only person in the room to share our thoughts. It is a question that could be answered if we weren't worried that the authenticity of our response would create distance between us and our colleagues. It is this fear of conflict that transforms a perceived problem in the present into a much larger issue down the line, particularly when we allow that fear to both dictate and mandate our behaviors.

Conversational Prompt: Awareness

1. Does fear of conflict exist in your organization?
2. If yes, what are the impacts of these behaviors?
3. If not, what have you done as an organization to ensure that it is understood that conflict is not always inherently negative, but rather a response to being made to feel empowered and safe enough to share a unique perspective?

While fear of conflict behaviors impacts all library workers, they take a particular toll on marginalized, minoritized, or racialized staff. For these groups, the resistance to engage due to fear of conflict creates false narratives and perceptions. Under the guise of fear of conflict, those who are brave enough to speak out against injustices, exclusionary behaviors, or internal policies that are damaging to communities of color may find themselves managed by individuals who would rather push them into the margins, ignore them, or worse, overlook their contributions. Perhaps the most detrimental aspect of resistance to fear of conflict for marginalized, minoritized, or racialized communities is the behavioral stereotyping that is often associated with advocating on one's own behalf. It's important to consider the intersectional impacts created by fear of conflict and how our individual identities shape and inform how confident or safe we feel in practicing self-advocacy.

How are we creating a sense of psychological safety for minoritized, marginalized, and racialized colleagues? Are we demonstrating that they may feel comfortable expressing opinions without fear of repercussions or retributions? For far too many, operating under the confines of fear of conflict may be the only place where they hold space. Marginalized, minoritized, or racialized colleagues may work in environments where they have been told that conflict is deemed divisive or rude. Or, as the singular member of a minoritized, racialized, or marginalized group, they may feel powerless to move the needle. The choice to act outside of or within the constructs of fear of conflict is both complicated and nuanced, particularly when the implications of voicing an opinion or remaining silent may create unfair and unwarranted narratives about whether you are a valued member of the team.

In environments where fear of conflict is centered, those who don't practice these behaviors are often mischaracterized as "combative" or a "threat." And, even as these individuals are often forced to decide whether the benefits of collective or self-advocacy are worth the professional risks, those who hold power and operate under the parameters of fear of conflict may operationalize tactics that enforce silencing—effectively eliminating a marginalized, minoritized, or racialized staff member's ability to create their own narratives about the impact of fear of conflict on their working lives.

When it comes to fear of conflict for these colleagues, the lessons that we've learned about community and, more importantly, **allyship and accompliceship** should inform our willingness to disengage from this dangerous form of silencing. We must ask ourselves if the fear of creating a platform for minoritized, marginalized, or racialized communities is that they will speak their truth. Perhaps the fear lies in the realization that the sharing of these truths will call attention to larger, more pervasive concerns that amplify and reflect disproportionately inequitable outcomes for success that exist in our organizations.

> **Conversational Prompt: Accountability**
>
> 1. How are minoritized, marginalized, and racialized communities impacted by fear of conflict in your organization?
> 2. What safeguards have been created to ensure that an internal culture rooted in fear of conflict doesn't silence minoritized, marginalized, or racialized communities?
> 3. What mischaracterizations of individuals who are outspoken exist in your organization? Is fearlessness of conflict viewed as positive or negative?
> 4. Consider your own organizational practices. In what ways is fear of conflict part of your professional narrative?

When it comes to fear of conflict, there is often a misconception that if we own and address the behaviors, we can completely eradicate the conflict-averse responses that exist in our organizations. The idea is that the ownership of the behavior is the ultimate solution to transforming the behavior. This is, however, an unrealistic interpretation. Beyond our recognition of the many ways that fear of conflict exists in us and our organizations, there must be an approach to addressing our responses to the behavior itself. And while these steps begin with recognition, they also require the integration of implementation, communication, and sustained effort.

One of the most effective ways to practice the implementation of this process is to start by reframing the ways we view conflict in our libraries. Doing this requires us to consider what we've been taught about the role of conflict in our organizations. Take a moment to consider what you've learned about conflict in your own organization. Is conflict viewed as a challenge to your organizational mission, vision, or values? Or, is it viewed as an opportunity to share a varied perspective or idea? Our internal approaches to the idea of conflict inform staff responses to the process of idea sharing. What if we began framing conflict to challenge our fixed mindsets and work toward a common goal of identifying the best and most effective solution? How might this challenge or transform our fear of conflict-led responses?

Along with the implementation that demystifies conflict in our organizations, introducing an effective communication plan that works in alignment with the implementation plan is key. Communicating to our staff or colleagues that conflict isn't inherently negative may start with the introduction of staff-wide conflict resolution training. Introducing conflict resolution training is a great first step toward creating a starting point for the work ahead. In these spaces, staff are encouraged to develop awareness of their own feelings and perceptions, along with building emotional intelligence—the skills that enable them to recognize and empathize with the feelings and needs of others. More often than not, the fear of conflict is driven by our inability to effectively communicate our feelings or perspectives.

We can also communicate that fear of conflict is not standard practice in our libraries by making idea sharing an integral part of organizational practice. This can be introduced through the development of staff feedback forms or positive reinforcement for colleagues who share their ideas, particularly those related to policy or procedure. To create openness and communication about the concept of conflict, there must be an organizational commitment to equipping staff with the tools needed to engage in difficult conversations.

While we each play a key role in combating fear of conflict in our organizations, library leaders are integral to the success of this process. For leaders, this starts with acknowledging their own behaviors related to the fear of conflict. Leaders who are afraid to address issues with staff are ill-equipped to resist the temptations of remaining conflict-averse. Leaders who refuse to view conflict as a value-add miss opportunities to encourage and inspire innovation and boldness in their teams.

Sustaining efforts that challenge the fear of conflict will require that leaders focus less on what they believe is the "right" way to respond to difficult situations in favor of setting the expectation that even the most challenging ideas or perspectives won't go unaddressed. Departmental or team meetings are a dynamic way to build opportunities for leaders to encourage the sharing of varied perspectives or ideas. I have implemented a practice for encouraging difficult conversations that I call a Lemon Squeeze. Guided by rules of engagement, a set of communication guidelines that we all agree to adhere to, Lemon Squeezes allow staff to share ideas or concerns free from judgment or critique. When leaders create space for difficult dialogue, they demonstrate that healthy conflict can be effective, and that there is no reason to be fearful of it.

> **Conversational Prompt: Action**
>
> 1. How will you nurture recognition, implementation, communication, and sustained effort in your organization?
> 2. What one thing might the leaders in your organization do to transform an internal culture guided by fear of conflict?
> 3. Consider the aspects needed to challenge the fear of conflict: recognition, implementation, communication, sustained effort. Which aspect of this work do you find most difficult?

Tips for a Lemon Squeeze

If you're looking for opportunities to transform perception about conflict, try engaging your teams in a Lemon Squeeze. To begin this process, try the following:

- Develop a clear set of communication rules. Consider those rules that highlight listening and respect.
- Set a timer. The purpose of the Lemon Squeeze is to share perspectives, but there should be time-bound parameters. Keep track of time and hold the person sharing accountable.
- Be consistent. Once you've added the Lemon Squeeze to your meeting agenda, keep it there. To cultivate trust and foster psychological safety, it is important to demonstrate that the Lemon Squeeze is prioritized.
- Lead from the Background. Lemon Squeezes shouldn't be started by the manager. These moments are designed to encourage staff to speak and managers to listen.

8 Defensive Maneuvers

White Supremacy Work Culture Characteristic: Defensiveness and Denial

> **Warning Signs for Defensiveness and Denial**
> - Battle fatigue
> - Attrition
> - Resistance to change or ideation
> - A loss of community

The act of change isn't always easy. And one of the most difficult aspects of this process is our acknowledgment that there exists something within (or outside of) our **sphere of influence** that needs to be approached differently. For many of us, rethinking the way we've been doing something can sometimes feel less like progress and more like an admission of defeat. And while, in theory, we understand that the transformation born of change is the harbinger of innovation, advancement, or growth, our individual responses to change are uniquely different and impacted not only by the change itself but also by the circumstances surrounding that change.

At times, just thinking about the idea of change can give us pause. And, add to that the feelings and emotions that are invoked by the actual process, and you've got what can be a recipe for full-blown anxiety. When we allow our perceptions and fears to inform our view of change as a reflection of vulnerability or inability, we exhibit traits of the White Supremacy Work Culture characteristic known as Defensiveness and Denial. Over the course of our lives, we've all been defensive or recognized defensiveness in someone. It is a trait that exists in each of us, particularly since defensiveness is often informed by a wide range of experiences and emotions. However, how it shows up in our working lives is something altogether different.

When demonstrated in the workplace, defensiveness is exhibited through protective practices like avoidance and blaming that are designed to uphold current internal structures. Defensiveness presents as a refusal to meet for a debrief to discuss the future of an existing project, or, as an inability to assume ownership of an unsuccessful venture. In our library spaces, defensiveness exists as a distraction, an attempt to hamper communication and derail progress. Whenever defensiveness is present, there is also denial. Defensiveness is the act of avoidance; denial is an act of refusal. In our libraries, we most see the refusal of denial show up as the inability to acknowledge failures that exist in our internal structures.

In Chapter 2, we discussed the practice of perfectionism and its reliance on an organizational culture where winning and the ideals of right and wrong are prioritized. Defensiveness and denial as practices rely heavily on the ideas and behaviors of perfectionism. We see examples of this in library workers who are conditioned and taught to believe that their organizational or departmental ideas, solutions, or processes are perfectly designed at the onset. Used in concert with perfectionism, defensiveness and denial inform an approach to library services that is designed to hamper progress and maintain the status quo. The impacts of a culture of defensiveness and denial show up as:

- ☐ Making excuses for internal systems and structures.
- ☐ Low to no consequences for abuses of power, particularly if the individual holds power.
- ☐ Having to work around or despite individuals to advance efforts.

The behaviors exhibited when we are operating in spaces of defensiveness and denial are almost always connected by the throughline of avoidance. In our libraries, avoidance shows up when, despite the clear recognition that an internal policy, procedure, or service isn't effectively meeting the needs of our patrons, we choose the path of least resistance—to ignore or overlook. It is the removal of a title from the collection or canceling of a program—not because of the inherent danger of the library material or program concept, but because of the pervasive fear that exists around having to explain oneself.

Defensiveness and denial show up as a pair, testing our ability to fearlessly receive constructive feedback and derailing our ability to see or value new ideas and perspectives.

In libraries, there exists a fear of acknowledging defensiveness and denial. What we lose in our reticence to examine why change or transformation is professionally triggering for us is the opportunity to begin unpacking how we, as libraries and library workers, view the process of organizational transformation. How might we begin to view change as less of a trigger warning, and more of an opportunity to more fully embody our promises to our communities?

> **Conversational Prompt (Awareness): How Change Informs Defensiveness and Denial**
>
> 1. Are defensiveness and denial traits that you recognize in yourself? If yes, how do you address these behaviors? If not, what do you do to ensure that defensiveness and denial aren't behaviors you practice?
> 2. When opportunities for change are shared in your organization, are they welcomed? Or are they met with defensiveness and denial?
> 3. Can defensiveness exist without denial? Can denial exist without defensiveness? How might these two ideas work individually in your organization?

As a librarian and DEI practitioner, I've been privileged to work with many libraries to embed Diversity, Equity, and Inclusion (DEI) into the fabric of their organizations. As part of our work, I often like to begin by sharing the traits of white supremacy culture developed by Tema Okun—reframing them through a library lens. Inevitably, when I begin, there is a lack of recognition and skepticism over the likelihood that these traits could exist in their organizations. But inevitably, as we continue unpacking each trait, skepticism is replaced with recognition as participants begin to see a clearer picture of how these traits exist within the microcosms of their own library lives.

But, over time, I've noticed that something interesting happens when I begin discussing defensiveness and denial. Participants get quiet and stop sharing. This is a direct response to the fear of conflict that exists in us as library workers. On a more insidious level, this reaction, which I've come to recognize and expect, is the unspoken acknowledgment of the toxic culture of silencing. When silencing is present, there is also an environment where avoidance, protective measures, and perfection-seeking behaviors associated with defensiveness and denial coexist.

We must also consider how defensiveness and denial thrive in situations where there is an imbalance of both power and positionality. While anyone can practice defensiveness and denial, those who hold greater organizational power may do so without fear of being questioned or asked to stop. For those whose positionality doesn't afford them the carte blanche to practice righteous indignation without impunity, they may find themselves navigating a work environment where practiced silence is expected. And in those instances in which silence is not an option, the result is often retribution or retaliation for those brave enough to speak out.

The danger in the silence created by defensiveness and denial is that those who engage in the practice are committed to supporting and amplifying their own messages. Because of their positionality and perceived power, they are afforded the ability to speak more loudly, less objectively, and most impactfully. Scary, right? Now, imagine that this individual is a decision-maker who can support or derail important initiatives like building a strong equity practice. In these instances, defensiveness and denial can lead to an overall sense of powerlessness. But, as Francis Bacon famously said, "knowledge is power." The knowledge gained through a greater understanding of the power dynamics associated with defensiveness and denial helps us to begin thinking of ways to effectively regain our voices.

> **Conversational Prompt (Accountability): Power Dynamics and Defensiveness and Denial**
>
> 1. Which of the steps for addressing individual defensiveness and denial do you find most challenging? Why?
> 2. What might it look like for your organization to address defensiveness and denial? Where would you begin?
> 3. What might you do to ensure that the messaging supported through the practice of defensiveness and denial doesn't have a lasting impact on morale (personal and organizational)?

So how do we navigate in environments where defensiveness and denial exist? Addressing these behaviors requires us to employ the following steps:

Step 1: Understand How the Behavior Is Showing Up.

What do we mean when we say that someone is acting defensively? Are these behaviors marked by words, actions, or both? As a first step in identifying defensiveness and denial in our libraries, we must determine what this looks and feels like in our working environments. Does it appear as interrupting colleagues when they're speaking, or justifying the response to a problem? Maybe it's showing up as body language that reflects anger or frustration. It's important to note that for one individual, interrupting may be a sign of enthusiasm or interest, while to another, it is considered the ultimate show of defensive behavior. Taking the time to better understand how the behavior is showing up can better prepare us for the next step in this process.

Step 2: Authentically Acknowledge

Once we can recognize how defensiveness and denial are showing up, it's important that we acknowledge our awareness of the behaviors. Acknowledgment should not be used to excuse defensiveness and denial, but rather as a practice of empathy. When we find ourselves working with people who frequently demonstrate the traits of defensiveness and denial, it's difficult to extend them grace—particularly if you've been on the receiving end of the scapegoating and blaming that often accompany these behaviors. Phrases like "I'm sorry you're frustrated" or "I recognize that you've put a great deal of time and effort into this" are two examples of affirming statements that can be used to acknowledge a person's feelings or experiences. And while using these statements may not prevent a person from practicing defensiveness and denial, they will serve in de-escalating a situation.

Step 3: Reframe and Reshape

Defensiveness and denial are most dangerous when the person practicing these behaviors single-mindedly chooses to focus on a perceived loss instead of viable solutions. When recognizing this singularity in others or ourselves, it will require us to shift our focus. We do this by working individually or collectively to reevaluate what the next steps could look like. This may start with questions like, "What might it look like to start again?" or "How can we honor what was good about our project, while innovating to make it great?"

Step 4: Direct Is Best

Just because you are choosing to lead with empathy in your interaction with someone who frequently employs defensiveness and denial, it doesn't mean that you are a pushover. In fact, it takes a great bit of confidence and fortitude to hold space for people who seem to be determined to find fault more often than not. There is, however, a requirement that empathetic conversations also be direct conversations. This means that even as we acknowledge the feelings and experiences of the person exhibiting defensiveness and denial, we make clear our own concerns about the impacts of the behavior in a way that is concise, fact-based, and non-accusatory. A dynamic way to apply this practice is to use "we" statements and not "I" statements as a way of underscoring the importance of a shared commitment or team effort. Here are a few examples of "we" language in practice—"It is important that we embrace change, because it impacts us all." "We all worked hard to develop our outreach program, but it's time that we develop new strategies for success."

On an individual level, the characteristics of defensiveness and denial are detrimental to the success of our library initiatives. When defensiveness and denial are applied more collectively in our libraries, we demonstrate to our communities that we aren't listening, that we view change as a perceived threat, or that we only value a high-level approach that limits our ability to authentically see and address front-facing issues or concerns.

But most importantly, defensiveness and denial work in concert with other white supremacy work culture characteristics like perfectionism and One Right Way thinking to inform the community's perception that the library is neither interested in nor invested in what the community most values and needs. And while there are no library utopias where defensiveness and denial are non-existent, we can work toward cultivating a culture in which we are able to view the constancy of change and transformation as the welcomed value add that they are.

Taking this "value-add" approach has allowed libraries to more deeply consider the equity, diversity, inclusion, and belonging of our spaces, to reimagine our approaches to collection management and development, and to develop programs and services that, quite simply, delight people. What we lose when we allow defensiveness and denial to "win" in our organizations is the natural curiosity and ingenuity that make this possible.

> **Conversational Prompt (Action): Taking the Necessary Steps**
> 1. Consider the four action steps for addressing defensiveness and denial. How might you build your capacity in each of these areas?
> 2. As an organization, what might be done to create openness around discussing the impacts of defensiveness and denial?
> 3. **Scenario:** During an all-staff DEI training, a colleague expresses open frustration over having to participate. "Why are we doing this?" "We're always welcoming." Using the four action steps as a guide, how might you address this act of defensiveness and denial?

9 Stretched and Stressed

White Supremacy Work Culture Characteristic: Progress over Process

> **Warning Signs for Progress over Process**
> - Quantity over quality
> - Impact may not match effort
> - Change management concerns
> - Staff who lack agency

One of the joys of my life is being an avid gardener. Over the years, I've found it to be a practice that is just as fruitful for the soul as the body. There is something quite peaceful about weeding, mulching, or watering in anticipation of watching something grow. Like most gardeners, I've learned many tricks and tips for harvesting and growing bountiful fruits and vegetables, with some suggestions working better than others. But one of the biggest lessons gained from gardening is that the growing **process**—the proper planting, the watering, and the soil preparation—and the **progress**—bounty and health of the harvest—are inextricably tied. Without the consistency of the sustained processes used as part of my growing methods, my progress would be nominal at best.

Understanding the balance between process and progress isn't limited to the practice of gardening; the significance of understanding the intersections between these two ideas is also key to cultivating and maintaining a balanced work culture. As with my garden, when we can apply our understanding of process and progress in our libraries in equal measure, the yield tends to be an organization that is running synergistically—setting goals and expectations that are aligned. When we don't value process and progress as equal entities, we find organizations that prioritize the ideas of success, innovation, and recognition over the needed steps to ensure that the pursuit of these goals is strategic, lasting, and most importantly, non-damaging to staff, patrons, or community.

The demonstration of these behaviors in our organizations is rooted in the white supremacy work culture behavior known as progress over process. Believe it or not, the conflation between the ideals of progress and the necessity of process shows up in our libraries more often than we would care to admit. It is the rushing of the rollout of systemwide initiatives so that we're able to say that "we did it first," or completing tasks and procedures at breakneck speed because there is a sense of overwhelm created by an internal culture that favors how quickly we work over the quality of the work. We also see the undertones and overtones of progress over process show up in our libraries as:

- ☐ Encouraging staff to take on more.
- ☐ Uncomfortable trade-offs that go with proposed growth.
- ☐ Taxing staff or volunteers emotionally and physically to reach a goal.
- ☐ Leaving staff unprepared to effectively support a new policy, plan, or initiative.

One of the most detrimental aspects of a progress-over-process culture in our libraries is the physical and mental toll that it takes on library workers. When progress is prioritized over process, there is an almost expected sense of urgency. In Chapter 4, we discussed how a created sense of urgency in our organizations can lead to staff taking on more responsibility in the hopes that they will be seen as valued contributors to the team. Organizations that create a sense of urgency alongside the behaviors of progress over process foster an internal culture where staff aren't individually able to decide if they want to take on more but are collectively encouraged by library leadership to do so. Progress over process in our libraries promotes a lack of agency; it asks that library workers forget everything they've learned about doing things the most effective way in favor of doing them the faster way. What we lose when we engage in progress over process is the clarity created through a shared understanding of a process and the efficiency gained by being allowed to take our time to do something well.

> **Conversational Prompt (Awareness): How Progress over Process Shows Up**
>
> 1. Imagine a process that is integral to the success of your work. Now, consider being asked to skip, overlook, or remove this step altogether. What are the impacts of this request?
> 2. In what ways does progress over process exist in your organization?
> 3. How do you (individually) ensure that you aren't prioritizing progress over process in your working life?
> 4. In what ways does your team or organization address and acknowledge instances in which the outcome is favored over the process? What might you like to see done differently in these instances?

Understanding how progress over process exists in our library spaces is just the first step. Our work toward transforming these practices requires that we are able to identify how progress-focused behaviors show up in our organizations. If you were to ask most people who drive process-focused behaviors what their goal was in engaging and sustaining these practices, most would respond: **growth**. This is often because we are taught that progress and growth go together, and without one, you cannot have the other. After all, isn't growth a good thing?

The fact is that progress-focused growth in our libraries can often be a double-edged sword. In theory, growth proves organizational success. And, for libraries, it signals both the significance of their role in the community as well as the long-term viability of library services. This is particularly powerful in a world where libraries are under attack, and so many appear not to understand our mission or values. But when progress is prioritized over process in our libraries, there is often a hidden agenda, a behind-the-scenes environment in which the quest for growth can tax resources or foster burnout.

These behaviors are particularly detrimental in our libraries when the desired progress-focused goal relies on the active participation of staff who are already working to keep up with a growing workload and service demands. When progress over process exists as a function of perceived success, library workers are made to own the responsibility of bringing projects or initiatives to fruition, even when the projects have unrealistic timelines or unspoken expectations. Often, this forced ownership may require staff to tax themselves to the breaking point, working and doing more to an end. These instances have lasting impacts, harming both mental and physical health. Progress over process in organizations isn't autonomous; for staff, there is no choice but to add to already full professional plates. In these spaces, library workers are made to feel both the anxiety and disempowerment created by the knowledge that the feelings of overwhelm in their organizations are both normalized and expected.

The singularity created by a progress-focused organization is often unsustainable. Holding ourselves and our libraries accountable for practicing progress over process requires that we are honest and transparent about the impacts that our initiatives may have. What do we gain from the practice of engaging in rapid expansion? What is gained from a more demanding service model? And will a focus on quantity over quality be of benefit to our staff or communities overall?

> **Conversational Prompt (Accountability): In Pursuit of Growth**
>
> 1. Is our library focusing only on short-term wins, or are we also considering the steps needed to be successful in the long term?
> 2. How often are we working in reverse to fix errors caused by the race toward progress?
> 3. If asked anonymously, would staff say we value process or progress?
> 4. How has progress over process affected hiring and retention?
> 5. Is our library known for moments of rapid growth and success that are followed by slow periods where shifting and regrouping are needed?

It is important to acknowledge that progress is needed in our libraries. After all, progress inspires the innovation that supports our organizations in introducing programs, services, and supports that both delight people and meets them where they are. Along with innovation, progress, if implemented with care, can inspire library workers to become more agile, open, and unafraid to try something new. But perhaps one of the biggest benefits of progress is that it allows our libraries to focus on the people-focused aspects of our work, adapting to the ever-changing needs of our service communities. For these and many other reasons, there is a place for progress in our organizations.

Progress is most successfully created when we are better able to understand and integrate processes as part of our plans. And this starts by recognizing that progress and process are balanced concepts. Viewing process as an integral part of progress requires us to define and establish a clear plan that identifies a path forward, indicators of success, and workflow methodologies. Libraries that are singularly focused on progress risk starting and restarting projects or initiatives multiple times. Conversely, organizations that are only process-focused may not be open to taking risks or making needed changes. Striking the right balance between progress and process requires engaging in the following planning steps:

Step 1: Be clear about our goals and how we will achieve them.

Step 2: Identify the processes needed to successfully support a desired goal.

Step 3: Determine who operationalizes these processes.

Step 4: Decide on a tool or method that will support process implementation and progress-focused achievements.

Step 5: Monitor progress through a continuous feedback loop

Step 6: Foster a culture of openness to making necessary changes.

Progress-over-Process Exercise

Directions: Practice the steps shared above for bridging progress and process by completing the questions below. The questions may be completed individually or as a team.

The project I wish to achieve is _____.

The organizational progress gained through the completion of this project is _____.

The processes needed to ensure successful project completion are _____.

The project management tools I will use are _____.

Bridging process and progress for my project requires that I/we _____.

In addition to implementing the aforementioned steps, the shift from progress over process will also require that libraries build a culture of process ownership. Helping library workers better understand the value of processes helps to support overall organizational progress-focus. Building this understanding can be implemented through training experiences that teach library workers the skills needed to better understand current processes and evaluate areas of improvement. What we gain when we make process the foundation of our progress-focused initiatives are library workers who can operationalize with both a greater understanding of what is needed to meet goals and an enhanced recognition of existing factors that may function as impediments to progress.

> **Conversational Prompt (Action): Creating Balance between Process and Progress**
>
> 1. In what ways might you rework your current processes to better align with your progress-focused initiatives?
> 2. Consider the steps for striking a balance between process and progress. What do you currently do well? Where is there room for growth?
> 3. Does your organization prioritize progress, process, or both? How do you demonstrate this?

Progress over process is a constant that we navigate in our working lives. It exists because libraries understand just how significant innovation and advancement are to our service model. It often feels like our reputations are on the line, and in an ever-changing world that increasingly questions our value, libraries also must change. But even as we work toward progress, it is important that we take the time to ask ourselves what the costs of over-prioritized progress are for our libraries and library workers.

How are we "tending" our professional gardens? Are the fruits of our labor—students, staff, patrons, community—receiving what they need to fully thrive in our libraries? Or are we missing critical steps in our growing process by prioritizing what we believe to be progress over the processes needed to ensure that we're able to fully meet and sustain our missions, visions, and values? To make the shift from being progress-first to progress-focused organizations, libraries must decide what's most important to the communities we serve: being responsive or being reactive. Making the right choice will make all the difference.

PART 3

Shifting Our Views of Professionalism

Throughout the previous chapters, you've been asked to challenge the assumptions, beliefs, and behaviors that inform professionalism in libraries. As library workers, challenging the construct of professionalism requires that we ask and consider three questions: How do we define professionalism? How does it define us—both individually and organizationally? And, who decides what professionalism is and what it looks like?

Asked alone, these questions are quite simple and direct. But asked together, each of these questions has much deeper implications that require us to stop, think, reflect, and consciously transform our approach to the ideal of professionalism.

Acting in support of this transformation can also be supported by practicing and integrating a set of supporting behaviors that are designed to act as tie-ins to support how we stop, think, reflect, and consciously transform.

Engaging in this transformation work requires that we:

Consider power dynamics: Believe it or not, imbalances of power often inform our understanding of or commitment to certain standards of professionalism. We see this show up in our libraries when those individuals who hold more power—whether positionally, experientially, or through tenure—use this power to introduce standards of professionalism that they feel are necessary for the overall success of the organization. The danger in this is that unchecked personal power dynamics can create inequity and inaccessibility. Taking the time to evaluate organizational power dynamics can amplify the ways in which the influence and insights of a respected few may have far-reaching impacts that inform standards of professionalism in an organization.

- **Center transparency and inclusion:** Reevaluating our approaches to professionalism requires that we practice openness around the ways that professionalism has been interpreted and practiced in our libraries. It also requires that we welcome new voices to the decision-making process, inviting more perspectives to have a seat at the decision-making table. Centering inclusion allows us to create dynamic shifts in our approaches to creating a library culture where all staff feel they are deciding with, instead of being decided for.

- **Communicate:** The practices of fear of conflict, progress over process, and defensiveness and denial can create in us an aversion to discussing ideas and behaviors that could be holding back our individual and organizational progress. This could involve developing and communicating a clear set of practices around both leading and engaging in difficult conversations. It could mean inviting community conversations to discuss professionalism with all staff. It's important that communication is guided by a clear set of rules of engagement that both set the tone and create a safe space for all participants.

- **Practice self-reflection:** Much of the work that we do in service of organizational excellence requires that we start with ourselves. In fact, when it comes to the fear of conflict, defensiveness and denial, and progress over process-focused behaviors that accompany WSWC approaches to professionalism, our ability to turn inward and self-reflect can redefine our approach to how we work. Cultivating our ability to better understand what creates professional comfort or discomfort isn't always easy. But, it starts with our ability to more thoughtfully consider what professionalism means to us as individuals. It invites us to consider how we wish to be viewed as library workers and to reset or reimagine the parameters that we've allowed ourselves to be taught about our individual and collective value to our patrons, our communities, and to our libraries.

Evaluate Efforts: How do we know if we are consciously transforming our organization's approach to professionalism? To ensure the accountability, transparency, and lasting change that we wish to see, it is vital that an evaluative process is introduced. Operating solely with our recognition that fear, lack of trust, burnout, and impostor syndrome are created when unrealistic standards of professionalism are introduced is not enough. For our libraries, conscious transformation requires that we do the work of identifying inconsistencies in our policies and determining where ambiguity exists throughout the life cycle of the decision-making process. Beyond this, evaluating our approach to professionalism helps us to measure its impacts, allowing us to more clearly identify new pathways to defining professionacmpowering us with the information that we need to navigate along the way.

Allowing ourselves to think critically and authentically about those behaviors that make us feel valued and valuable in the workplace can transform our approaches to professionalism. How will you ensure that the long-held standards of professionalism that exist in our organization—and the fear of conflict, defensiveness and denial, and progress over process that inform these standards—won't impact the way you show up in the workplace?

Consider power dynamics: What stories are the power dynamics in your organization telling?

_____
_____
_____
_____
_____

Center transparency and inclusion: Who must you include in conversations about professionalism?

_____
_____
_____
_____
_____

Communicate: How do we ensure that our messaging about professionalism isn't informed by defensiveness and denial or fear of conflict?

_____
_____
_____
_____
_____

Practice self-reflection: What am I doing to transform my own values and perspectives around the practice of professionalism?

_____
_____
_____
_____
_____

Evaluate Your Efforts: In what ways have we shifted our views of professionalism? What have been the impacts of these shifts?

_____
_____
_____
_____
_____

Understanding how professionalism has informed the practice of library services is foundational in helping us to set intentions and boundaries for ourselves as library workers. Let's continue to build upon this foundation in Part 3, where we will discuss the importance of showing up authentically and the white supremacy work culture behaviors that stand in the way of us doing so.

10 Showing Up Authentically

I love attending library conferences. For many reasons—the learning engagement, the opportunities to connect with colleagues, and the seemingly endless supply of tote bags (as if I need one more). But one of the things I value most about library conferences is witnessing the varied representations of identity that the library workers in attendance represent. There, all together in one space, we are able to fully capture the many similarities and differences that exist between us. But even as I marvel at the wonderfully nuanced aspects of my fellow library workers, I can't help but recognize that there still exists a sense of interconnectedness between us all.

Over time, I've come to realize that this is what psychological safety looks and feels like. What I am recognizing when I see the fullness through which my fellow library workers represent themselves is the beauty that exists in an environment with people who recognize that in a convention center—with other library folk, we are expected to show up authentically as who we are.

But what happens after the library conference? Does the same welcome to show up fully exist in the libraries where we work? Are feelings of acceptance, understanding, and connection still prioritized? Often that answer is yes, but for others, the answer might be a resounding no. In fact, many of us are still navigating work environments in which our identities aren't seen or fully valued. Sometimes our libraries feel like exclusive clubs with only our identities as library workers receiving invites for admission. While our professional identities are welcomed, the other aspects of ourselves—including our ideas, experiences, interests, or style choices—are not. Working in environments where we're only welcomed to bring parts of ourselves can feel performative, disheartening, and exhausting. And as with most exclusive clubs where limitations are placed on who can or cannot show up, when those aspects of ourselves that are required to "stay home" aren't in attendance, the overall experience just isn't as enjoyable.

While it can feel altogether discouraging to compartmentalize who we are in our working environments, the good news is that we can do the work of more fearlessly owning our identities—and we do this through cultivating the practices of embodiment and intentionality. Embodiment is informed by our conscious decisions about living in the fullness of who we are—it is the authentic practice of bringing our whole selves with us, wherever we go. Alongside this practice is intentionality, which is the demonstration of the processes and practices that we use to reflect our understanding of who we are.

Building our understanding of embodiment and intentionality prepares us to do the work of better understanding others, as well as ourselves. As library workers, building our capacities around embodiment and intentionality helps us to create opportunities for trust building and authentic engagement. And, these practices teach us to operationalize empathy, supporting colleagues in being themselves.

As we prepare to discuss the value of showing up authentically and the White Supremacy Work Culture behaviors that are fostered through our inability to do so, it will be important to consider the ways in which we, as library workers, are both embodying who we are and intentionally and completely reflecting our awareness of who we are through our actions and behaviors.

It's equally important to think critically about what our libraries are doing to support library workers as they show up authentically. This will require libraries to challenge the ideas of culture fit and sameness that often exist in our organizations. They must understand that an individual's identity and experiences can act as catalysts for creativity and innovation. It is vital that libraries recognize the significance of promoting shared values and working together in pursuit of a common goal. Not sameness, which silences staff and sends an unhealthy message that diverse perspectives are, in some way, inherently wrong.

Over the next three chapters, I ask that you consider the ways in which you practice embodiment and intentionality. Recognizing what we need to feel fully supported when we show up is vital to our success as library workers. Moreover, the significance of this recognition is magnified by how we demonstrate to those around us that we are present.

Let's prepare for the chapters ahead by thinking about our own embodiment and intentionality.

Conversational Prompt (Intention):

1. On a scale from 1 to 10, how safe do you feel showing up authentically to work?
2. What informs how you will show up at work?
3. How do you support your team or colleagues in fully showing who they are?

Conversational Prompt (Embodiment)

1. How do you reflect your decision to show up authentically to the workplace (ideas, style choices, values, etc.)?
2. How might you use the practice of embodiment to create opportunities for trust building and authentic engagement?
3. Does authenticity matter in the workplace? Or should we carefully decide which aspects of ourselves we share with our colleagues?

11 No "I" in Team

White Supremacy Work Culture Characteristic: Individualism

> **Warning Signs for Individualism**
> - Tendency to believe in workplace meritocracy
> - Undervaluing the work or efforts of colleagues
> - "Othering" when asked to engage in team-based efforts
> - Competition over Cooperation

Can the work of meeting the mission of our libraries be accomplished by one person (for all of the solo librarians out there, I know that answer is sometimes yes)? Or, are we strengthened and fortified through the recognition that our efforts, initiatives, and services are made better through our collective work? It's difficult to imagine the work of libraries without considering the many connections we build in service of our communities. But we can't overlook the impact of the White Supremacy Work Culture known as individualism on our library ecosystems.

Individualism is a practice that suggests that each person should think and act independently, rather than depending on others. And, if we're honest, this is something that many of us have been taught is the pathway to success. Perhaps someone has said to you, "keep your head down, do the work, and focus on being your best." For many of us, the practice of individualism is the primary mechanism by which we measure our professional achievement.

When individualism becomes a standard practice in our libraries we risk losing our grasp on team-centered collaboration, choosing to close ourselves to the opportunities and experiences of learning with and from others. Rather than working together toward a common goal, we alienate ourselves in favor of establishing our own best courses of action. Individualism on a team or in a department can impact morale and create division amongst colleagues. If the person engaging in individualism holds a position of power, it can create damaging information silos that leave staff in a perpetual state of frustration.

Because individualism informs our approaches to personal goals, achievements, and sense of personal autonomy, there is no singular practice. In some instances, individualism may show up in the behavior of a colleague who is so singularly invested in their own ideas that they are unwilling to entertain those of others. It may appear as overconfidence or a lack of interest in the ideas of others. Maybe you recognize in a colleague that there is a healthy distrust in others' ability to contribute, meet deadlines, or effectively complete a project.

Individualism's approaches to thinking and acting independently can often be confused with the practice of individuality. But it is critical that we understand that these two practices are not the same. Individualism is exclusionary and asks that we only act in service of ourselves. While individuality also requires us to act in service of ourselves, it is an inclusive practice that both honors who we are and invites others to better know us. Individuality is showing up authentically, creative risk-taking, non-conformity, and the joy of knowing who we are as part of a larger community. Individualism narrows our perspective and deemphasizes organizational collaboration and connection in favor of cultivating a team of one. The impacts of individualism show up in our libraries in the form of:

- [ ] Discomfort or inability to work in a team setting.
- [ ] Singularly valuing top-down approaches to leadership.
- [ ] Devaluing group feedback in favor of individualized positive feedback.
- [ ] Prioritizing individual success over collective progress.

Individualism can also be used as a form of protection that we use to distance ourselves from challenging work experiences. Instances of this could include navigating a difficult work environment where there is low trust, or using individualism as a form of protection when feeling overlooked, under-utilized, or unseen by co-workers or managers. But using individualism as a safety net doesn't protect us from the existence of problems. More often than not, it only serves to create more distance between the person practicing the behavior and their team. As library workers, our commitment to a shared vision makes individualism a high-stakes behavior that threatens our ability to provide much-needed services and support to the communities we serve.

> **Conversational Prompt: Awareness**
> 1. In what ways does individualism inform the way you work?
> 2. Have you noticed displays of individualism in your organization? What do they look like?
> 3. Individualism can create information silos. How might these silos show up in your library?

One of the most challenging aspects of individualism is its impacts on team-centered collaboration. Personal achievement is inextricably tied to the practice of individualism, and those who lean into individualism do so because they want to be valued for their own merit. And while the desire to be valued for our contributions is a desire that most of us share, those who find personal achievement through the lens of individualism find it difficult to share praise or commendations for a job well done. This inability to enjoy collective success may result in diminishing the efforts of other colleagues or driving competition between colleagues as a means of advancing their own efforts.

But perhaps the most damaging consequence of individualism is the practice of **othering**, or making someone feel intrinsically different from oneself. Othering as a practice of individualism can be exercised as a means of devaluing the contributions of colleagues and silencing the sharing of ideas. Along with these intended impacts, the person practicing individualism can shift the narrative of the planning efforts to support their own initiatives or goals. The individualism-specific othering that can occur in a team setting not only disempowers all team members, but can have particularly lasting and harmful impacts when experienced by minoritized, racialized, or marginalized colleagues who have systematically been ignored in the workplace.

When individualism is used as a method of othering, it is important to stop and address the behavior. Choosing to ignore it, or waiting until the "right time," will only serve to affirm the behavior.

We interrupt these behaviors by:

1. **Creating Awareness:** Make clear the language and approach used in the practice of othering. Be sure to provide any needed context— **Sample Language:** I want to stop the meeting here because you said (repeat back to the individual what was said).
2. **Name Impact:** Be clear about the impact of the othering practice. Don't make assumptions about the intent; focus on the feeling invoked by the words.
3. **Sample Language:** What you said/did was harmful for the following reasons (always provide clear examples)
4. **Repair and Rebuild:** Create space for the person who practiced othering to apologize. Equally important is allowing space for the person who experienced the othering to forgive. The apology can happen via email or in person. But there must be a mandate of accountability. It is important that the person who has been othered isn't expected to forgive right away. They deserve all the time and space they need to process their feelings or thoughts.

    Sample Language: I'd like to give you an opportunity to apologize for what was said. You may do this via email or in person.

    Sample language for the person who was othered: Please know that you are supported. And, even as we've asked for an apology on your behalf, there is no timeline for your forgiveness.
5. **Institute a restorative practice:** Always consider what restoring trust, community, and collaboration may look like for the team. Consider the best course of action to ensure that lessons are learned. This may look like inviting more authentic conversations about what teamwork should be, or specialized sensitivity training.

> **Conversational Prompt: Accountability**
>
> 1. How do you ensure that individualism doesn't impact team-based collaboration?
> 2. How do you demonstrate that we value our staff/colleagues for their own merits, while ensuring that we're also amplifying group achievement?
> 3. What are the strategies that you've developed to address individuals who devalue the efforts of their colleagues/teams?

Shifting our approaches to individualism in libraries doesn't require us to practice groupthink or deprioritize the individual successes of our colleagues or teams. Rather, it asks that we cultivate our ability to hold space for others. The act of holding space asks that we remain present with those around us, allowing them to be who they are, free of judgment. For those who engage in individualism, holding space challenges that person to demonstrate that they are present by listening to someone else's experiences.

We hold space when we recognize the practice of individualism in a colleague who is fearful of working collaboratively. We hold space when engaging with a community partner who has prioritized the recognition of their organization over their partnership with the library. We hold space for leaders who are so determinedly focused on receiving the accolades for a project that they've forgotten to acknowledge those who've contributed to its success. Holding space requires a great deal of compassion and care. And while it takes time and effort to build our capacities in the practice, it can have a transformative impact on those who authentically commit to doing the work.

As individual contributors, we each hold value by giving of our time and talents to our organizations. When I consider individualism and libraries I think of the many instances in which colleagues have worked alongside me toward a common goal and the collective feeling of accomplishment that we felt in equal measure. If I am working in service of myself and my colleagues are also working in service of themselves, then who is working in service of our communities and their ever-present needs?

Conversational Prompt: Action

1. Have you recognized instances of competition over cooperation in your library? What might you do to address this?
2. What does building your capacity in holding space look like for you?
3. Finding the middle ground between collectivism and individualism is important. What does this middle ground look like in your organization?

12 Honoring Complexity

White Supremacy Work Culture Characteristic: Binary Thinking

> **Warning Signs for Binary Thinking**
> - Inability to see the duality in a situation
> - Attempting to further an agenda based on limited information
> - Sense of urgency

In preparing a new library worker for their first day at the circulation desk, I once observed their manager say "if a patron asks you to do something that I haven't taught you to do, simply say no. We live or die by the policies—they are our protection." This statement was met with tremendous reverence, with the new employee vigorously nodding in agreement. But what stuck out most for me was this: "we live or die by the policies." While both I, a proverbial eavesdropper, and the new employee both knew that life and death weren't on the line, we clearly understood the underlying message—that when it came to library services there were only yes's or no's. And herein lies the problem that libraries have with the White Supremacy Work Culture behavior known as Binary Thinking.

Binary Thinking is a form of cognitive bias that limits our understanding of the world around us to two opposing perspectives, which are considered either/or decisions—fact or fiction, wrong or right, or in the case of the story I shared about the manager who was training the new library worker—yes or no.

Whether libraries engage in Binary Thinking consciously or unconsciously, understanding the complexities of taking an either/or approach to library service is something that we must think critically about. If we are consciously engaging in approaches that aren't people-centered, then what has informed this choice? And, if the behaviors are unconscious, or implicit, what messaging have we, as libraries, received over time that has informed the development of ineffective service models informed by an intentional inflexibility?

These behaviors, whether conscious or unconscious, are informed by mental shortcuts, which are processes we use to make it easier to understand information. The mental shortcuts created by Binary Thinking are informed by our desire to make the decision-making process as straightforward as possible. But even as we attempt to create this ease of access for others and ourselves, our reliance on the practice of mental shortcuts can impact our ability to ensure that policies, services, or practices are more nuanced and inclusive. And although it is understandable that creating a bit of ease to support our often challenging roles is a welcomed respite, when that ease means that we favor the simplicity of an either/or approach over the substantive effort required to engage in creative problem-solving, we must do things differently. When we consciously or unconsciously practice mental shortcuts in our libraries this can lead to Binary Thinking behaviors that include:

- [ ] Seeking out a single solution to a problem.
- [ ] Engaging in bias or stereotyping.
- [ ] Fostering an us vs. them environment.
- [ ] Oversimplifying complex issues.

> **Conversational Prompt: Awareness**
> 1. Where does Binary Thinking exist in your organization?
> 2. Can you think of specific services, systems, supports, or policies in your organization that were created as a mental shortcut? (Mental Shortcuts: Method of creating ease of processing information)
> 3. Are the practices of Binary Thinking that exist in your organization conscious or unconscious? Why?

Beyond using Binary Thinking as a default behavior to make decision-making easier, there are far greater and more damaging implications for libraries whose organizational frameworks are built upon a foundation of Binary Thinking. A more frequent consequence of this Binary Thinking is the creation of false dichotomies. As a practice, false dichotomies are created when we narrow our options by factoring for choices that can't or won't impact our decisions.

For instance, imagine a library deciding whether or not to become fine-free based on an imagined funding source that will cover the annual costs of fines. The false dichotomy that exists in this scenario is that there is a funding source that will cover costs. In creating this narrative, and focusing on the unlikely possibility of the imagined funding source, valuable time is spent discussing an idea that will never be. Beyond that, focusing on a false dichotomy can distract from conversations about a viable path forward. When it comes to false dichotomies and how they inform Binary Thinking it is important to recognize that the either/or decisions we make in our libraries will not always be rooted in something real or tangible. The danger of false dichotomies are the ways in which they distract us from being able to make truly informed decisions.

In addition to false dichotomies, Binary Thinking can also lead to approaches that can lead to rigidity. As demonstrated in the scenario I shared at the beginning of this chapter, rigidity in libraries is an outgrowth of Binary Thinking. Because we have been so conditioned to a binary service model with little room for gray areas, library workers may find it difficult to operate outside of the parameters of what we've been taught is the best course of action. In this way, libraries are equality-centered, ensuring that everyone gets the same level of service and support. But moving beyond Binary Thinking helps us to become equity-centered, an approach that encourages our libraries to move beyond our inability to adapt to change toward a model that honors and factors in individual needs and circumstances. For our libraries, this may look less like "living and dying" by the policies, and more like taking the time to better understand and factor in the ways in which our policies impact our patrons.

Binary Thinking prevents us from embodying the equity-centered practices that we'd like to build. Along with the stringency and rigidity that inform our stasis and inability to adapt, the all-or-nothing approaches to Binary Thinking are often demonstrated through acts of bias or stereotyping. In our libraries, this shows up when we categorize people based upon information that a colleague has shared with us, or by allowing a momentary observation to inform our ideas of what a person wants or needs, or what they will or won't do.

In these instances, we see Binary Thinking informing decisions of whether or not to trespass a patron, whether or not to present a program or offer a service, or whether or not to invite someone to have a seat at the decision-making table. The bias informed by Binary Thinking can show up in the form of "qualified" or "unqualified" assumptions that may have lasting impacts on the recruitment, hiring, or advancement processes. The act of categorizing used in many hiring practices fails to evaluate an individual's experiences, abilities, or potential. And, the long-term effects of making miscategorizations and assumptions in our organizations can inform homogeneity and prevent us from being reflective of the communities we serve. The good news is that we can challenge the practice of Binary Thinking that is informed by biases and stereotypes by de-prioritizing duality in our decision-making. This may look like introducing a more intentional hiring process that allows for deeper insights into a prospective candidate. Or by taking the time to thoughtfully interrogate colleagues when they are unable or unwilling to evaluate the gray areas. As a first step, start by considering if duality exists in your current hiring practices. And, if it does, begin planning for how you might change that.

> **Conversational Prompt: Accountability**
>
> 1. How might you ensure that you aren't factoring for choices that can't or won't impact your decision-making?
> 2. In what ways are you practicing stringency or rigidity in your organization? What informs this behavior?
> 3. What might shifting your practices from equality-centered (where everyone gets the same thing) to equity-centered (where everyone gets what they need to thrive) look like in your organization?

Asking library workers to learn to "work in the gray areas" can be like asking us not to breathe. But learning to embrace ambiguity not only helps us to become better decision-makers but also more informed ones. As an added benefit, embracing what might be perceived as middle ground can create a bit of respite from the persistent analysis paralysis that is created when we are asked to decide between the lesser of two choices. Throughout the chapter, I've mentioned critical thinking, which is the process of analyzing information to make a decision. When it comes to shifting our approaches to Binary Thinking, cultivating our ability to make informed decisions will be the approach that benefits us most.

Learning how to carefully and thoughtfully analyze information will help us develop more informed and intuitive policies. As library workers, it will better prepare us to assess the judgments that we make—ensuring that we operate free of the assumptions and miscategorizations exhibited through bias. But most importantly, building a culture of informed critical thinkers will ensure that we aren't continuing to impart the fear of the all or nothing, live or die approach to library work that prevents us from authentically doing the work we love.

Exercise: Moving beyond the Binary (Action)

Cultivating our ability to think critically can inform our approaches to Binary Thinking. The following actions are Keys to Critical Thinking. Using the Keys to Critical Thinking as a guide, consider how you will move beyond the binary by completing the prompts below.

Open-mindedness: In what ways do we make decisions that are driven by the awareness of the responses or perspectives of our community?

Questioning: When it comes to decision-making, do we ask necessary questions, or do we lean into the ease of processing information that comes from using mental shortcuts?

Reasoning: When false dichotomies inform strategies or policies in our organization, how do we redirect and re-center our team?

Communication: How are we clearly and effectively expressing our commitment to moving beyond the duality and rigidity of Binary Thinking in our messaging? How are we inviting creative thought and perspective in the development of content across all communication platforms?

Awareness of Bias: How might we enhance or transform the decision-making process by seeking out diverse perspectives?

Emotional Intelligence: In what ways do I recognize the impacts of Binary Thinking on my work? How do I recognize its impacts on those I work with?

13 The Comfort of Privilege

White Supremacy Work Culture Characteristic: Right to Comfort

> **Warning Signs for Binary Thinking**
> - An inability to "get comfortable being uncomfortable"
> - Overgeneralizations
> - Creating toxic environments for those who speak up and make you uncomfortable

How do you define comfort? Is it a feeling, an idea, a place? Like most things, the idea of comfort and being comfortable is a highly nuanced construct, with each of us determining for ourselves how to define our own psychological, physical, or social aspects of comfort. Beyond this, the idea of being comfortable has been ever-evolving, shifting and changing with modernity. But even as our ideas around comfort change, the desire to be comfortable remains unchanged. Understanding the role that comfort plays in our lives is important because it helps to shape the ways in which we embrace life's challenges, changes, or experiences. Developing this understanding will also help us to better respond to those moments where discomfort exists and we find ourselves disempowered to change it. When we view the ease and freedom of comfort as an expected practice, we are engaging in the White Supremacy Work culture behavior called Right to Comfort.

One of my favorite mantras on this matter can be credited to author, speaker, and digital strategist Luvvie Ajayi Jones. In her now-famous TED Talk, Ajayi Jones encouraged the audience to "get comfortable with being uncomfortable." I must admit that I had to sit with these words for days after I watched her TED Talk. I knew that beyond Ajayi Jones' challenge to the audience to authentically share their opinions and be fearlessly honest, there was so much more meaning behind her speech. For me, the true takeaway from her talk is that being comfortable doesn't always help us grow, but being uncomfortable does. As library workers, it's vital that we consider whether or not we will decidedly prioritize comfort over being "uncomfortable." But most importantly, we have to do the work of better understanding why we believe ourselves to have a right to comfort and how the assumption of comfort informs our behaviors as library workers. When our behaviors are informed by a Right to Comfort, they show up as:

- [ ] People in positions of power who require complete emotional and physical comfort.
- [ ] Prioritizing personal interests over organizational needs when engaging in project work.
- [ ] Individuals may incorrectly compare and conflate a lack of personal comfort with the experiences of oppression, marginalization, or unfair treatment experienced by BIPOC.

> **Conversational Prompt: Awareness**
> 1. What are some things that create discomfort for you in the workplace?
> 2. How likely are you to address these issues?
> 3. What stops you from saying something?

While Right to Comfort behaviors can show up in any of us, at any time, they are particularly dangerous when operationalized by those with positional power. In such positions, organizational leaders may expect to get their way, without question. Additionally, they may be resistant to questions or demonstrations of uncertainty, viewing them as challenges to their authority. When those with positional power choose to center Right to Comfort, it creates environments where staff or teams are unable to authentically express concerns or share dissenting perspectives. In rare instances when staff embolden themselves to do so, their concerns are often invalidated. Led by a desire to be made comfortable, library leaders can create an internal culture where staff are afraid to challenge ideas for fear of retribution. And, guided by a perpetual state of ensuring the Right to Comfort of library leadership, staff and teams work at the mercy of leaders who believe themselves to be infallible.

In our libraries, Right to Comfort can have damaging impacts on internal culture and morale. It looks and feels like spaces where we are unable to authentically express concerns and ask questions because there is a culture of silencing. And, where silencing exists, there also exists a deeply rooted undercurrent of frustration and hopelessness. In recognizing how Right to Comfort is made manifest in our organizations, it is critical that we amplify the four-letter word that we hope never exists in any of our organizations—fear. Fear is a byproduct of Right to Comfort, existing in both the person who is demonstrating the behaviors and the person who is on the receiving end of their actions. As library workers, Right to Comfort behaviors can show up in any of us, at any time. But when these behaviors are practiced by those who have positions of power, they can have top-down impacts that reverberate throughout the organization.

The fear response elicited by Right to Comfort shows up in many ways. In peer-to-peer interactions, it may show up as fear of accountability, demonstrated through a constant avoidance of owning and acknowledging work left undone. Right to Comfort, rooted in fear response, may have internal to external impacts, where staff may unconsciously view the library as an exclusionary "safe space" for some, but not for all. This may look like a disproportionate number of trespasses for an unhoused patron, or the leveling up to bring in security or police support when feeling threatened, or more dangerously, uncomfortable. We must recognize that Right to Comfort exists as a mechanism that we weaponize in libraries to excuse our inability to admit our fear and apprehension in dealing with uncertainty or unfamiliarity. In the most unfortunate of circumstances, when fear and Right to Comfort intersect, patrons representing marginalized, racialized, or minoritized communities are often most impacted.

Beyond baseline fear, the Right to Comfort is also demonstrated through a desire to avoid conflict at all costs. This behavior, known as fear of conflict, is characterized by an inability to acknowledge or address challenging situations or have difficult conversations. Guided by fear of conflict, library leaders may create an obligatory culture in which staff work hard to preserve and protect the leaders' feelings, having been conditioned to believe that addressing conflict creates discomfort. For staff or teams, the preservation of the feelings of a manager can act as a forcing function for accepting ownership of perceived mistakes, even when they didn't make them. Staff may also become fiercely loyal, as they work to protect the feelings of a manager, or conversely, resentful that they are unable to authentically express feelings of frustration or ask difficult questions.

The tiptoeing effect created by leaders who operationalize fear of conflict can inform the development of a team that is both unprepared to meet challenges and unable to accept feedback. And, for the leader who refuses to recognize the inherent value of channeling conflict into opportunities for growth, there exists an ever-present sense of avoidance that fails to benefit both the leader and their team.

It is important to note that fear of conflict doesn't only exist in leaders or managers. It is a behavior that transcends positionality. Fear of conflict in staff can exist in interactions with colleagues, making it difficult for an individual to self-advocate or express dissenting opinions. And, it can also show up through our interactions with the communities we serve. Right to comfort that is informed by fear of conflict can lead us to believe that patrons should act in service of our needs and expectations. In these instances, we are unable to see everyday human conditions like frustration, fear, or failure as anything other than challenges to our ability to work comfortably throughout the day. And, in having to acknowledge the behavior of a patron who has experienced trauma right before entering the library, our right to comfort has been tested or challenged. It is important that in considering the impacts of the right to comfort and its ability to create fear of conflict, we, as library workers, recognize that comfort is rarely guaranteed, and it is certainly not promised.

> **Conversational Prompt: Accountability**
>
> 1. In what ways have you expected the right to comfort in the workplace? What were the impacts of these expectations on your team/colleagues?
> 2. Fear is a byproduct of the "right to comfort." When faced with a challenging situation, what might you/your team do to address the fear and apprehension that comes with navigating uncertainty or unfamiliarity.
> 3. When was the last time you experienced fear of conflict? What did you do to address this fear?

As library workers, it is vital that we understand that our expectations of guaranteed comfort can create a hierarchical imbalance between us and the library user. In centering ourselves, the message that we send to our communities doesn't speak to the welcome and belonging that we say we create in our libraries. If your library commits to an organizational focus on building multilingual collections, but staff consistently demonstrate discomfort in engaging patrons for whom English is a second language, there is a clear disconnect between the messages being sent by the library and the internal behaviors of staff. When library workers say they believe in restorative practices and empowering patrons but then lean heavily into asking for assistance from security as a means of "handling" difficult patrons, a crisis of comfort arises where the only person who finds solace, safety, or security in the library becomes the library worker. And while it is important to acknowledge that there are myriad of circumstances in which library workers require assistance as a means of their own safety and security, there are also many instances in which the comfort of having these resources may lend itself to increased or excessive use of this form of power.

Shifting our perspective on the Right to Comfort in libraries must begin with an authentic assessment of how we view comfort—starting with unpacking why we believe ourselves to be more deserving of solace, ease, and safety than the communities we serve. It will require us to consider how the right to comfort is demonstrated at an organizational level through our community partnerships, policy development, collections, and services. Most importantly, we must recognize that organizational behaviors are largely informed by the people who work for our organizations. Imagine the impact of an expressed right to comfort by everyone you currently work with. How might it impact both internal and external interactions? The right to comfort exists in an organizational or individual desire to ensure that the systems that they associate with safety and ease remain unchanged. The challenge of this behavior is that it negates the ability of others to feel that same sense of ease and safety.

Along with evaluating how we view comfort in our libraries, we also must consider what we lose in prioritizing comfort. The prioritization of comfort may lead to stagnancy, limiting our ability to see ourselves as viable and vibrant contributors to the success of our communities. The fear that is inherently and inextricably tied to right to comfort behaviors can impair our ability to question or challenge perceptions of libraries or library services—preventing us from acting as respected advocates for our work. A particularly damaging consequence of prioritizing the right to comfort are the power imbalances that are created between library worker and patron, manager and team, or library and community.

What might leaning into discomfort do for our libraries and for us as library workers? For our organizations, it may mean recognizing that everything we do won't always have a clear purpose or agenda. In doing this, we may discover that what we perceive as being in a state of disorganization or flux may prove to be the exact thing we need to move the needle from discomfort toward change and innovation. Can you think of a time when your organization has successfully supported staff through feelings of uncertainty or discomfort in pursuit of a perceived lofty goal? When staff are uncomfortable, successfully operationalizing for change in our organizations requires us to honor the natural fear response that comes with shaking things up. It requires organizational level-setting to ensure that staff understand that while the journey toward what's to come may be unknown, there is a clear destination.

As library workers, we lean into discomfort by honoring that we won't always understand or be able to control everything that is happening around us. In fact, at times, we may feel frustrated or afraid of our inability to make the decisions that most impact us. Leaning into discomfort may come through the realization that we can't control the thoughts, behaviors, or perspectives of those around us as a means of making us feel secure or safe and that the identities and experiences of others shouldn't be weaponized against them when they don't agree with us or their shared truth makes us uncomfortable.

Making the shift from right to comfort for organizations and library workers comes with the requirement that we recognize that what makes us comfortable may not always make us successful, impactful, or community-focused. What we gain from our willingness to challenge our capacity to act meaningfully—even when navigating discomfort—is a greater understanding of how to share agency with our communities, colleagues, and communities, and not hoard it.

Conversational Prompt: Action

1. Have you had a professional breakthrough born of discomfort? What did you learn from this experience?
2. Does an expectancy of comfort exist in your organization? Your team? In what ways is the right to comfort showing up?
3. Prioritizing the right to comfort can create tremendous power imbalances. Consider the ways in which the right to comfort may show up in the following relationships.

   Colleague to Colleague: _____
   Leader/Manager/Admin to Staff: _____
   Library to Patron/Community: _____
   Library Board to Staff: _____
   Library to Community Partner: _____

4. What does a sharing agency look like in your organization?

14 Our Path Forward

We began this journey by learning that in order to better understand and change the behaviors and manifestations of White Supremacy Work Culture, we needed to practice Awareness, Accountability, and Action. The momentum gained through the practice of each of these steps allows us, as library workers, to both unpack and pack up those behaviors that have enabled us to create false narratives around our profession and encouraged us to act fearfully and not fearlessly in our approaches to work in this field. Examining the behaviors of Perfectionism, Worship of the Written Word, Sense of Urgency, Individualism, Right to Comfort, Binary Thinking, Defensiveness and Denial, Progress over Process, and One Right Way are necessary steps in reimagining library culture. In addition to the recognition and transformation that is born of our ability to develop awareness, accountability, and action around those systems or processes that may not be in our best interests, saying no to white supremacy work culture asks that we challenge what we believe are certainties, giving ourselves the permission to more deeply examine those ideas or behaviors that feel uncomfortable or uncertain.

As we engage in this work, it is important to acknowledge that our efforts will fall on a continuum with changes on both a macro and micro level. Change on a macro level for your library may look like a complete reimagining of your internal approaches to worship of the written Word with a focus on building a more inclusive approach to ensuring that the information shared and prioritized in your organization includes both verbal and non-verbal formats. And yet, for another organization, change on a macro level may simply be the admission that white supremacy work culture is something that exists and needs to be both acknowledged and addressed. No matter the size or scope of our efforts, the common thread between them is that there must be an existing willingness to change.

When I think about the existence of white supremacy work culture in our libraries, this is one of the biggest challenges we face. For our libraries, changing our culture and behaviors starts with managing our approaches to the process of change. Over the years, I've engaged in a myriad of change models to support the shifting of mindsets on both an individual and organizational level. And while the selection of a change management tool can be subjective, I've found that the The Prosci ADKAR Model and Lewin's Change Management Model have been instrumental in guiding organizations as they question what they know for sure. What makes these two models complementary in change work is that The Prosci ADKAR Model is a dynamic tool to support individual reflection and commitment to lasting transformation and Lewin's Change Model can be operationalized to support collective change for an organization.

The Lewin's Change Model presents a clear but effective three-step framework that asks organizations to consider change as a process that requires them to **unfreeze**, **change**, and **refreeze**. During the unfreeze stage, an organization prepares for the work ahead—this includes considering what needs to be changed along with identifying why the suggested change is necessary. An unfreeze stage for your library, through the lens of dismantling White Supremacy Work Culture, may look like a comprehensive analysis of the ways that its behaviors are showing up and informing decision-making practices. The second step, or "change" phase, encourages organizations to begin thinking critically about implementing change and the complementary processes needed to make that change successful. This phase encourages creative thinking and ideation, inviting stakeholders to join in the act of identifying a solution. Beyond analysis, engaging in the change phase to address White Supremacy Work Culture might look like introducing the concept of Design Thinking—a human-centered approach to problem-solving and innovation—with staff to catalyze the processes of idea development and idea sharing. The final phase of the Lewin's Change Model asks that an organization "refreeze." During this pivotal phase, an organization is asked to both implement the ideas and practices developed during the unfreeze and change phases, integrating patterns of consistency that inform a sense of stability and stasis. The process of refreezing is a foundational practice that encourages an organization to set and maintain intention. Applying this final step to an examination of White Supremacy Work Culture behaviors should be demonstrated through marked internal shifts that are observable and unmistakable. The beauty of the Lewin's Change Management Model is the lack of ambiguity that exists in each of its steps. But while this change model is seemingly straightforward, its success relies heavily upon the practice of organizational vulnerability and introspection, and this isn't always an easy process. **What existing behaviors in your organization might benefit from unfreezing, changing, and refreezing?**

We know that the success of organizational efforts is determined by the workers who inform and shape internal culture. For this reason, change management for individual transformation is equally beneficial to the implementation of long-term organizational goals. The Prosci ADKAR Method ® is a change model that can be used to guide impactful change on an individual level. ADKAR is an acronym for Awareness, Desire, Knowledge, Ability, and Reinforcement, and each of these outcomes is key to the successful implementation of change. Through their engagement with ADKAR, individuals are taught to adopt a set of skills that better prepares them for the fear, anticipation, and unpreparedness that often accompany change. The benefits of applying the ADKAR method to understanding White Supremacy Work Culture are that it allows individuals to process through their resistance to internal change by addressing their own existing behaviors. I encourage you to try the ADKAR method by using the template below to consider your own capacity to address White Supremacy Work Culture.(See Figure 14.1.)

Now, more than ever, libraries and library workers find themselves at the intersection of challenge and change. There are so many threats to our organizational futures, but just as many (if not more) reasons that we must do the work of preparing ourselves to be steadfast and immovable. And while being steadfast and immovable doesn't mean that we're unchanging—it does require that we become unwavering in practices that de-center the learned white supremacy work culture behaviors that hamper our ability to be the diverse, inclusive, equitable, and accessible organizations that we'd like to be.

If this book has provided you with ah-ha moments—instances in which you were able to recognize the behaviors of yourself, your colleagues, or perhaps your organization reflected back to you—then we're on to something good. I've committed my professional life as a librarian to working against systems of inequity and injustice, so to share with you what I know for sure, and have that information in some way resonate with you is what one of my dear friends calls a "big, audacious hope." But I want to take a moment to address the person who

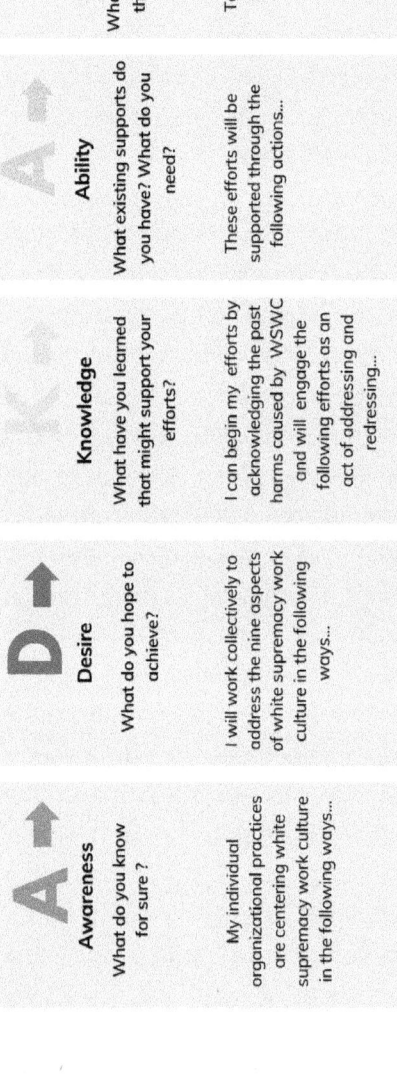

Figure 14.1 *ADKAR Change Model Exercise. Source: Christina Fuller-Gregory.*

may not know how to unpack what they've read, or where to begin. One of my favorite writers, activist Adrienne Maree Brown, writes in her book *Emergent Strategies* that "small is good, small is all, the large is a reflection of the small."[1]

This idea that the act of starting an effort is equally as important as the change that results from completing it is transformative. The implementation of what you've learned from this book will require you to consider those efforts, both large and small, that you will carry forward.

Early on, you were asked if you were:

- ☐ Ready to acknowledge, address, and redress the ways in which white supremacy culture exists in your library.
- ☐ Prepared to challenge the professional behaviors that we've long held as the standards of excellence.
- ☐ Excited to create a more inclusive and culturally proficient working environment, believing that libraries are dynamic institutions that can (and should) exist beyond the historical and foundational.

Now that we've come to the end of the book, let's reframe these questions through a reflective lens.

- What have you discovered about the ways in which white supremacy culture exists in your library?
- In what ways are you prepared to challenge the professional behaviors that we've long held as the standards of excellence?
- What most excites you about creating a more inclusive and culturally proficient working environment?

Hopefully, you're now able to answer these questions with clarity and purpose. And, if not, perhaps you're able to better identify behaviors (individually or organizationally) that you'd like to address. Changing the cultures of our organizations is the responsibility of all library workers—there are no hierarchies in change work. And whether those efforts are large or small, it is important that we honor our participation in the process.

Creating change begins with each of us. **What does starting "small" look like for you? Your organization?** And, in recognition that nothing happens without a start, **what do you need to gain momentum**? The work begins NOW.

Note

1   Adrienee Maree Brown, *Emergent Strategy* (Chico, CA: AK Press, 2017).

Appendix

Chapter 4: "No Time to Spare" Scenario Answers
Scenario 1: My Problem Is Your Problem

Dr. Jenn Fowler, a tenured member of the Music Department faculty, often uses library resources. She often uses the library to prepare for auditions, including researching music compositions, making copies, and laminating.

1. **Question:** Is Dr. Fowler creating a sense of urgency?

   Answer: Yes, this is a classic case of a colleague not meeting their personal deadlines and creating added work for you to meet their goals.

2. **Question:** Who is affected by Dr. Fowler's behaviors?

   Answer: Everyone.
   - Dr. Fowler's reputation, as her lack of self-awareness and recognition of her persistent sense of urgency, impacts her relationships with library faculty/staff.
   - Staff who are burdened to either act upon this sense of urgency or fear that they haven't been responsive to a patron/tenured member of staff.
   - Library department administrators are impacted as they are on the receiving end of complaints from Dr. Fowler, and library faculty and staff who have reached out for guidance about how to properly respond to these frequent requests.
   - Students who are potentially asked to leave class to pick up materials are not only missing class but have a sense of urgency created for them to say "yes" to Dr. Fowler's requests.

3. **Question:** Who might feel disempowered to address this sense of urgency?

   Answer: Staff and students may feel disempowered to say something about this behavior. There is clearly a power dynamic at play here.

4. **Question:** How might you address Dr. Fowler?

   Answer: Remember the Four Steps to Addressing a Sense of Urgency
   1. Respond to the behavior in the moment.
   2. Detail why the behavior creates a sense of urgency.
   3. Clearly demonstrate through example the impacts of the behavior.
   4. Come prepared to present an alternative.

Scenario 2: The Rush to the Finish Line

Recently, you were asked to act as a project manager for a community partnership that would provide Wi-Fi to an underserved community.

1. **Question:** In what ways do you note a sense of urgency?

   Answer: There is "race to the finish" behavior demonstrated in this scenario. We're often so excited about the potential for positive press that it can cloud our judgment. In this case, the project manager has not only chosen to abbreviate the timeline but has also limited the participation and the varied perspectives that are a part of a participatory process.

2. **Question:** Who might be affected by this sense of urgency?

   Answer:
   - Community members who don't have the benefit of a library staff member sharing with a working group their knowledge of the unique needs that they may have. Beyond this, no one in the community was asked to engage in the process.
   - Library staff at the community branch expressed that their opinions were not valued or respected.
   - The project manager, who down the line will learn through staff and community feedback about the missteps associated with this rushed process.
   - The "selected" team members have been made pawns in this process and have been chosen specifically because of their **positionality**.

3. **Question:** What might the library staff at the community branch do to ensure that they aren't excluded or silenced during this process?

   Answer: Consider the Four Steps, but instead of developing the content to directly address the project manager, broaden the scope and share the response to this behavior with those in the **sphere of influence** who have the power to enact change.

Scenario 3: I'm Growing and Tired

Khari, an early career librarian, hasn't stopped since their first year as a librarian. They currently serve on two internal committees, plan all adult programming for their location, and have recently become active with their state's library association.

1. **Question:** How is a sense of urgency showing up in this scenario?

   Answer: What we're seeing here happens often. Khari has set unrealistic expectations for himself as a means of building professional or personal momentum.

2. **Question:** Who is creating the sense of urgency? Khari? The library?

   Answer: In this instance, it all comes down to Khari. While it's difficult to say no, it's imperative to create healthy boundaries, and in their haste to be the best, Khari is not doing this.

3. **Question:** What emotions or feelings are you sensing in Khari?

   Answer: There are lots of emotions here: excitement for the opportunities, apprehension to say no, fear of not living up to expectations. And, although they are not there yet, eventual frustration or anger at feeling overworked.

4. **Question:** How might they continue a trajectory of success while addressing the sense of urgency?

   Answer: As mentioned in this chapter, set and feel safe in prioritizing boundaries for your own professional well-being. You don't have to share these boundaries with anyone; simply know them for yourself and remain committed to holding true to them.

5. Question: How might Khari's manager be more mindful of fostering a sense of urgency for the staff?

Answer: Good managers want to see the people they manage grow and excel. However, a good rule of thumb is to ask if a team member is interested in an opportunity. Once you've shared the opportunity with them, ask them to think about it, and give them a day or two to consider. Remember, we are working to combat a sense of urgency, and giving someone time to think supports those efforts.

Chapter 8: "Defensive Maneuvers"

Scenario: During an all-staff DEI training, a colleague expresses open frustration over having to participate. "Why are we doing this?" "We're always welcoming."

Using the four action steps as a guide, how might you address this act of defensiveness and denial?

Step 1: Understand How the Behavior Is Showing Up
Consider what you observe or notice in the behaviors demonstrated by your colleague. Note body language, tone of voice, emotion, or feeling.

Step 2: Authentically Acknowledge
While you are not obligated to agree with the person speaking, authentically acknowledging requires us to center empathy. An example response might be, "While I understand that we are welcoming, participating in this training allows us to build upon that welcome."

Step 3: Reframe and Reshape
Instead of allowing the speaker to co-opt the positive energy in the space, find ways to shift the focus. This may sound like, "We are all invested in ensuring our welcome. We have an opportunity to learn new ways to engage our patrons."

Note: It is important to use "we" language and not "I" language. This acts as a reminder for the individual that they are part of a team.

Step 4: Direct Is Best

Be empathetic and direct. It is important that you do not allow an individual who has decided to practice defensiveness and denial to co-opt the learning space. Try language like this: "While we would love to have you participate fully in the training, we understand if you do not wish to participate. However, the rest of the team will continue the learning process."

Index

accomplliceship 58
accountability 4, 7–8, 15, 107
action 4, 8, 15, 107
ADKAR Method 109
Ajayi Jones, Luvvie 99
allyship 58
assumptions 96, 97
    "qualified" or "unqualified" 96
awareness 3–7, 15, 107
    of bias 98
    of perfectionism 15–16
    worship the written word 23

Bacon, Francis 66
Berg, Yahuda 26
Binary Thinking 93–8
    consequence of 95
    form of cognitive bias 93
Brown, Adrienne Maree
    Emergent Strategies 111
Brown v. Board of Education 6
bullying 15

Carnegie, Andrew 5
change management, for individual transformation 109
change stage, library 108
communication 97
    organizational behaviors around 26
    worship the written word, internal culture of 23
conflict resolution training 60

culture
    of perfectionism 20
    of process ownership 76

decision-making process 94
defensiveness and denial 63–9
    in libraries 65
    navigating environments 67–9
    power and positionality 66
    power dynamics and 66
Diversity, Equity, and Inclusion (DEI) 65
Du Bois, W. E. B. 5
Dweck, Carol
    Mindset 41

embodiment 84
Emergent Strategies (Brown) 111
emotional intelligence 98
equity-centered practices 95
equity lens 17
Ettarh, Fobazi 36–7

false dichotomies 95
fear of conflict 55–61, 101–2
    conflict resolution training 60
    effective communication plan 60
    Lemon Squeezes 60, 61
    in libraries 56–7
    misconception 59
    resistance to 57–8
    in staff 102
fixed mindset 8, 25, 41, 59
forced ownership 74
Fowler, Jenn 35

growth   73
growth mindset   41

individual accountability   4
individualism   87–92
   as form of protection   88–9
   impact in libraries   88
   in libraries   91
individualism-specific othering   89
in-group behaviors   15
intentionality   84
intent vs. impact   15, 55

Jackson Public Library   6

"knowledge is power"   66

Lewin's Change Management Model   108–9
Lewis, John   6, 7
librarianship   21
libraries
   desegregation of   6
   tunnel vision in   22
library-centric working environments   56
library conference   83
library workers   27, 100, 103, 104
   anxiety and disempowerment   74
   fear of conflict for   56, 57
   perfectionism   14, 18
Louisville Western Branch Library   6

marginalized   18, 22, 51, 57, 58, 101
mental shortcuts   94
Microsoft   32
Mindset (Dweck)   41
minoritized   18, 51, 57, 58, 101

miscategorizations   96, 97
mission fatigue   32

National Association for the Advancement of Colored People (NAACP)   6

Okun, Tema   8, 65
One Right Way   39
   and internal culture   40
   operationalize and optimize behaviors   42
   to partnership development and community building   44
open-mindedness   97
organizational accountability   4
organizational behaviors   4, 16, 103
   around communication   26
organizational culture
   around One Right Way thinking   43
   of perfectionism   13–20
organizational history   9–10
othered/othering   53, 89, 90

perfectionism
   awareness of   15–16
   culture of   20
   indicators of   14
   organizational culture of   13–20
   positive perception   16
   professional standards   15–18, 20
The Perfection Question exercise   19–20
personal achievement   89
Plessy vs. Ferguson   5
process   71
   balance between progress and   75

professionalism
  myth of   51–3
  standards of   51–3
professional standards   15–18, 20
progress   71
  balance between process and   75
progress-focused growth   73
progress-focused organization   74, 77
progress over process   71–2
  in libraries   73
Prosci ADKAR Model   108–10
psychological safety   83
public libraries   5, 6, 39
public-serving entities   6, 7

questioning   97

racialized   18, 51, 57, 58, 101
reasoning   97
refreeze stage, library   108
restorative practice   90, 103
Right to Comfort   99–105
  behaviors as library workers   100
  impacts on internal culture and morale   101
  in libraries   101, 103
  library workers   103, 104
  prioritization of   103–4

sense of urgency   29–30, 72
  in libraries   30
  organizational culture in   30–1
  steps of behaviors   32–3
  traits of   31
  in workplace   33–7
Separate Car Act (1892)   5
silencing   58, 65, 66, 89, 101

sphere of influence   63
Summer Reading program   39

team-centered collaboration   87, 89
three A's   3, 9, 15
Tougaloo Nine   6

unfreeze stage, library   108
"value-add" approach   69

vocational awe   36

White Supremacy Work Culture (WSWC)   4, 5, 7–8, 107
  Binary Thinking   93–8
  culture and behavioral change   107–8
  defensiveness and denial   63–9
  fear of conflict   55–61
  individualism   87–92
  One Right Way   39–45
  perfectionism   13–20
  progress over process   71–7
  Right to Comfort   99–105
  sense of urgency   29–37
  worship the written word   21–7
workplace
  sense of urgency in   33–7
worship the written word   21
  behaviors associated with   24
  built-in inequity in   22
  internal culture of communication   23
  risk of   22
  transforming behaviors associated with   27

"Yes, And" approach   43–4

About the Author

Christina Fuller-Gregory is a librarian and principal consultant with Fuller Potential, a consultancy that supports libraries in developing a strategic focus through an equity lens. Growing up in the Upstate of South Carolina as the daughter of a library administrator, Christina Fuller-Gregory always knew two things: (1) that she would never be a librarian like her mother and (2) that after attending countless library programs on the weekends, her least favorite place was the library. Luckily, an adult Christina discovered that she was wrong on both counts. She did, in fact, become a librarian like her mom, and libraries would ultimately become her Third Place. Today, Fuller-Gregory uses her lifelong relationship with libraries to inform her work as an equity-centered library leader. Christina has been recognized as an American Library Association's emerging leader, she's acted as a committee member and chair for numerous library committees, and was recognized for her work in the equity space by *Library Journal* when she was named a Mover & Shaker. She is a highly sought-after speaker and consultant, and her writing has been featured in numerous publications. Led by Fannie Lou Hamer's belief that "Nobody's free until everybody's free," Christina's research and writing is driven by a desire to see libraries develop strategies for weaving equity, diversity, and inclusion into the very fabric of their organizations.